$3 Meals Your Kids Will Love

Delicious, Low-Cost Dishes for the Whole Family

Ellen Brown

LYONS PRESS

Guilford, Connecticut

An imprint of Globe Pequot Press

To Ilan, Mira, and Lev Dubler-Furman,
the small folk who bring such great joy to my life

To buy books in quantity for corporate use
or incentives, call **(800) 962-0973**
or e-mail **premiums@GlobePequot.com.**

Lyons Press is an imprint of Globe Pequot Press.

Rice Krispies is a registered trademark of Kellogg's N/A Co.

Project editor: Jessica Haberman
Layout artist: Melissa Evarts
Design: Sheryl P. Kober

Library of Congress Cataloging-in-Publication Data

Brown, Ellen.
  $3 meals your kids will love : delicious, low-cost dishes for the whole family / Ellen Brown.
     p. cm.
  Includes index.
  ISBN 978-1-59921-890-8
1. Cookery, American. 2. Low budget cookery. I. Title. II. Title: Three dollar meals.
  TX715.B87177 2010
  641.5'55—dc22

                                                          2009046833

Printed in the United States of America

10 9 8 7 6 5 4 3 2 1

Contents

Chapter 1: Saving Money at the Supermarket   1

This chapter is your recipe for eating better for less money. Here are all the tips you need to stretch your food budget via strategies for using coupons, shopping sales, and shopping your own pantry.

Chapter 2: Cooking Healthy Meals for Happy Kids   18

By letting go of convenience products, you're sharing the philosophy of professional cooks, and you'll learn all the tricks of their trade as well as have some basic recipes to make life easier.

Chapter 3: Soup for Supper   34

Kids love slurping soups, and because soup is a one-utensil meal even young kids can feel grown up eating it. Here's a wide range of healthful and inexpensive soups, drawn from cuisines around the world.

Chapter 4: $1 Snack Attacks   60

Remember that your food budget isn't only for dinners; it's for everything you eat. These smoothies, whole grain granola bars, and dips are all loaded with flavor, and are so easy to make.

Chapter 5: Yankee Doodle and Noodles, Too   79

Here's a whole bunch of all-American favorites your kids will love, and many of them add new twists, so you'll find them more interesting, too. Lots of new takes on old friends like meatloaf abound.

Chapter 6: Say ¡Olé! Hispanic and Southwestern Dishes   113

Tacos, fajitas, and enchiladas, not to mention variations on chili, are always popular with kids. They're also healthful when you make these foods with fresh ingredients, like the recipes in this chapter.

Chapter 7: Mediterranean Madness   **138**

Twirling pasta on a fork is almost as much fun for kids as picking up food with their fingers, and you've got many pasta recipes from which to choose. But there's much more to the sunny cuisines of this region, and you can explore them all.

Chapter 8: Pizza Power   **172**

Pizza is actually a great food for kids to eat, and they love to eat it and maybe even to arrange the toppings themselves. There are myriad ways to top pizzas, some traditional and some innovative; they're all in this chapter.

Chapter 9: Dishes with Asian Accents   **195**

Kids love the fun of using chopsticks, or at least trying to use chopsticks, and they're used in all Asian cuisines. While the base of this chapter is delicately seasoned Chinese dishes, there are also some Thai, Vietnamese, and Japanese options.

Chapter 10: (Almost) Guilt-Free $1 Goodies   **220**

When a sweet treat contains fruit or vegetables, it's easier to rationalize feeding it to kids. Those are the desserts you'll find in this chapter, along with some basic recipes you should have around.

Preface

There's no question about it. It's really hard to be parents in today's world if you're trying to raise kids to like healthy foods. It's a constant battle, especially when those healthy foods have to be prepared on a strict food budget. That's why I'm here to help; I really mean it that these recipes are $3 meals your kids will love. And you'll love them, too. In addition to seeing your kids join the "Clean Plate Club," I've developed the recipes so that some spicy adult ingredients can be added to your portions of the meals. No more bland food just to keep the kids happy!

I understand what you're up against feeding your family. As we all know, it's the era of the Happy Meal. It's very happy for the fast food chains that fill tiny tummies with foods laden with fat, sugar, salt, and chemicals, and almost devoid of nutrients; but the "food" comes in a cute box with a toy inside. And how do you make an apple or a piece of real cheese seem exciting after kids have watched the multimillion-dollar ad campaigns for sugared breakfast cereals in DayGlo colors hyped by cartoon characters or clowns? Unless all television is banned, your kids are being bombarded by those persuasive messages.

Then there's everything you read about the skyrocketing number of children of all ages who are suffering from obesity, and all the studies about the detrimental effects of too much refined sugar in children's diets.

So there you are in the supermarket, propelling yourself through the aisles to gather ingredients for a healthy meal that will elicit the same high rank on the kids' fun scale as junk food. Not an easy task, to be sure—especially with the rise in food prices we're now experiencing and will continue to experience in the future.

The causes for this increase in food costs are many and varied, and the reasons are global and not just national or local. For example, if corn farmers in Iowa are selling their crop to ethanol producers, then the cost of the remaining corn—which is used to feed chickens and pigs as well as make the evil high fructose corn syrup that seems to be used in most processed foods—escalates proportionally, and that leads to increases in the cost of the animals that ate the corn. If people in China's growing middle class finally have enough money to include more meats in their meals, then the cost of meat will rise in all countries; it's the simple equation of supply and demand.

That's why we need to rethink our approach to meals our kids will love, and that's where the recipes in this book can make your life easier and your dinner hour more fun for the whole family. The concept uniting the varied titles in the $3 Meals series is that the way to cook inexpensively is to use only fresh, healthy, and natural ingredients. High-cost cooking is the result of buying processed convenience foods that are laden with chemicals; thus the motto of the series is "Cost = Convenience + Chemicals." The only canned items used in the recipes are minimally processed, like canned beans and diced tomatoes; there are no cans of "cream of something soup" in any recipe.

As a general rule it is safe to say that the more a food is handled by someone *other than you*, the more expensive it becomes. Carrot sticks are more expensive than whole carrots that take but seconds to peel and cut. Packages labeled "stew beef" are generally far more expensive, and of uncertain origin from the cow, when compared to the chuck roast sitting next to them. You'll find when cooking these recipes that there's no reason to use these value-added products once you learn it just takes a few minutes in the kitchen to do it yourself—and come out with a superior product, too.

I'm very confident in my abilities to develop recipes; I've devoted the past thirty years of my life to making the life of the home cook easier, and meals more delicious, with more than two dozen cookbooks. But creating dishes kids would love? In all honesty, my "kids" are happy when I pop the top off a can of cat food. My experience catering to human children was minimal.

Certainly, I could do extensive research on what kids love to eat, and that's what I've done. But I decided that academic studies were just that—academic. My answer was to enlist the aid of a wide range of *real* moms and dads around the country who have children of various ages, ranging from toddlers to teens. You'll see many references in *$3 Meals Your Kids Will Love* to the Parents Panel.

The Parents Panel, which I affectionately dubbed my "Kitchen Cabinet" in the e-mails we exchanged, approved concepts and helped me devise the foundation for these recipes. All agreed that picking up food in their hands was a great bonus to get kids to like a food, as were fun colors and shapes. Their kids liked foods they could scoop, so there are a number of dip recipes in the chapter on snacks.

They also admitted to "sneaking" more vegetables into meals by chopping them into tiny pieces, and they all like to cook ethnic meals as a way to introduce their kids to new cultures. That helped me to develop the structure for the book; the recipes are divided by ethnic influence. If your kids love Italian food but won't touch anything Mexican, you can ignore the chapter on Hispanic dishes.

What the Parents Panel also did was share with me the stress they feel when getting the meal on the table each night, and almost universally reported that having the kids "help" them was clearly more of a hindrance except for a relaxing weekend meal or when baking cookies. That's why these recipes do not include the participation of the kids.

The exceptions to this non-participation rule are, of course, cookies, but also pizza. It had never occurred to me that any kid might like to put Cheerios on a pizza, but someone on the Parents Panel told me her child did. By allowing a few Cheerios, she coaxed a lot of green peppers and mushrooms into the kid, so it was well worth it.

So, cookies and pizza are for that occasional relaxed evening or for the weekend. Otherwise you can scoot around the kitchen in your precious few minutes to yourself and try to be super-organized.

The actual amount of your time it takes to prepare these recipes is less than twenty-five minutes, and many are on the table in the same amount of time. Those that aren't ready in 30 minutes are cooking unattended, so you can read your kids a story—or, I realize this is pie-in-the-sky—have a few minutes to yourself.

Happy Cooking!

—Ellen Brown
Providence, Rhode Island

Acknowledgments

While writing a book is a solitary endeavor, its publication is always a team effort. My thanks go to . . .

All the wonderful real moms and dads on my Parents Panel who shared their wisdom and all their tricks for raising happy and healthy kids. This group includes my darling niece and nephew, Ariela Dubler and Jesse Furman, who are raising my beloved Ilan, Mira, and Lev Dubler-Furman; dear friends Edye DeMarco and Tom Byrne for sharing Emma Byrne's preferences with me; Laura Horowitz for telling me about Will's favorite foods; Sylvia Elsbury, my California pen pal, for her advice from raising George, Mary, and Celeste; and Ilana Ruskay-Kidd, who added the vegetarian mom's perspective from her cooking for Emma, Gabriella, and Daniel.

Mary Norris, editorial director at Globe Pequot Press, for so willingly picking up the mantle to serve as editor for this series.

Jess Haberman and Julie Marsh, project editors at Globe Pequot Press, for their guidance and help all through the production process, and Jessie Shiers for her eagle-eyed copy editing.

Ed Claflin, my agent, who had faith in the various iterations of this project, as well as for his constant support and great sense of humor.

Nancy Dubler, my great sister, for sharing the grandmother's perspective on feeding kids.

My many friends who shared their palates at tastings, favorite stories about feeding miscellaneous children, and tips for saving money.

Tigger and Patches, my furry companions, who personally endorse all fish and seafood recipes.

Introduction

The recipes in this book are a "win-win" situation if you're a parent wanting to cook healthier foods for your family *and* remain on a tight food budget. One of the secrets that the multibillion-dollar food industry wants to keep a secret is that you save money using fresh ingredients rather than chemical-laden processed foods. But now that secret is getting out, and all the recipes in this book are also proof that healthy meals can be greeted by cheers at the dinner table by even the most finicky of eaters.

The goal of the $3 Meals series is an ambitious one; this small amount of money per person—less than the cost of a large fast food burger or a slice of gourmet pizza—is for your *whole meal!* That includes the greens for your tossed salad and the dressing with which it's tossed. It includes the pasta or rice you cook to enjoy all the gravy from a stew. And it includes a sweet treat for dessert. So unlike many books that promise cost-conscious cooking, this book delivers it!

Before we focus on cost, however, let's talk about health. It may not be by accident that *convenience* and *chemical* start with the same letter. Chemicals are what convenience foods are all about; they are loaded up with them to increase their shelf life, both before and after being opened.

One of the rules of economical cooking is that the more processed a food is, the more expensive it is. These recipes are made with foods that are ingredients; at one time they grew from the earth, walked upon it, and swam in its waters. The most processing that has taken place is the milk of animals being transformed into natural cheeses. So when you're cooking from *$3 Meals Your Kids Will Love,* you're satisfying your body as well as your budget.

No one—kids of any age or their parents—needs the amount of refined sugar that is found in processed foods. A high sugar content is not just a part of sweets or junk cereals; it's in almost everything.

Any time you see the words *sucrose, glucose, dextrose, sorbitol,* or *corn syrup* on a food label, it's another way of saying *sugar.* In the nineteenth century, when there wasn't an obesity problem in America, the average American consumed 12 pounds of sugar per person per year.

By 1997 this figure was more than 150 pounds per person per year. That means that every day each American eats 53 teaspoons of added sugar. Measure that out in a bowl, and you'll not be as surprised to learn from the Centers for Disease Control and Prevention (CDC) that the level of childhood obesity has more than doubled in the last few decades!

Another culprit of processed foods is trans fats. Many products now proclaim that they have "no trans fats" right on the box, right? Look again. If the words "partially hydrogenated" appear in the ingredients, it means that some chemist at a food company took a polyunsaturated oil and pumped it full of hydrogen, and that creates trans fats; it's trans fats of the second generation.

But healthy kids must come from healthy parents. Studies on childhood psychology have revealed that imitation of what they see is important to children's development, especially what they eat. Kids are no dummies. They're not going to want the carrot stick if they see you eating a bag of potato chips. If your kids open the refrigerator and see a bowl of carrot sticks and a bunch of fresh grapes, it's from those foods that they'll choose for their snack.

If you're now thinking "I can't afford all this fresh food," it's time to think again. The foundation of *$3 Meals Your Kids Will Love,* as well as the other books in the $3 Meals series, is all the tricks I've learned in professional kitchens—including my own catering kitchen. Professional cooks learn to minimize waste; wasted food translates to lower profit.

That means that the onion peels and celery leaves that you might be throwing into your compost bin or garbage can now become an asset because you'll have them frozen to make stocks. And you'll know you have succeeded in waste-free cooking when, at the end of the week, there's nothing in the refrigerator to throw away! That's quite a feeling of empowerment, and along the way you've been eating like royalty on a peon's budget.

There are a few ingredient compromises taken to trim costs; however, these shortcuts trim preparation time, too. This is the first book I've written for which I used bottled lemon juice and lime juice in recipe development rather than freshly squeezed juice from the fruits themselves; I discovered it took a bit more juice to achieve the flavor I was after, but with the escalated cost of citrus fruits, this was a sacrifice that I chose to make.

The same is true with vegetables; many of these recipes call for cost-effective frozen vegetables rather than fresh. For vegetables such as the chopped spinach added to a soup or casserole, or the peas added to many dishes, it really doesn't matter. Frozen corn kernels have much more flavor than fresh except when it's local and in season, and the same is true for green peas.

I've also limited the range of dried herbs and spices specified to a core group of less than a dozen. There's no need to purchase an expensive jar of anise seed or dried marjoram that you may never use again.

On the other hand, there are standards I will never bend. I truly believe that unsalted butter is so far superior to margarine that any minimal cost savings from using margarine was not worth the trade-down in flavor. Good quality Parmesan cheese, freshly grated when you need it, is another ingredient well worth the splurge. You use very little of it, because once grated it takes up far more volume than in a block, and its innate flavor is far superior.

The same is true for using fresh parsley, cilantro, and dill. While most herbs deliver flavor in their dried form, these leafy herbs do not. Luckily, they are used so often that they are inexpensive to buy and don't go to waste—especially with the tricks I'll teach you on how to freeze them.

Each recipe in the book is annotated with the number of servings; it's a range because soups and stews can stretch so easily. Other annotations are for the amount of "hands-on" time you will be spending slicing and dicing the ingredients. While economy is a bonus with soups and stews, they do take more time to prepare than seasoning a whole chicken to roast in the oven or tossing some burgers on the grill.

The last annotation is for the time it takes between turning on the lights in the kitchen and sitting down at the table to enjoy your meal. Depending on the food being prepared, this can be as little as 30 minutes or up to 4 hours. But during the time the food is cooking, you can be doing something else.

Interspersed with the recipes are some boxes containing nuggets of kitchen wisdom, or some fun facts about cooking. I've been a cookbook author for more than two decades, and I want to share some tricks of the trade with you.

Chapter 1:
Saving Money at the Supermarket

The reason you're holding this book is probably because while one or two of you are earning the money to buy groceries, there are many more mouths chewing the food. Your food budget just isn't going as far as it did even a few months ago, and you need some new ideas. Then you're thinking ahead to when the small mouths at your table will be going to college, and saving money is an almost Herculean task.

The recipes in this book will help you eat healthfully and deliciously as well as economically, but my help starts here. If you follow the hints for trimming the grocery bill found in this chapter, you will have paid for this book in one week.

As you can well imagine, as a cookbook author I spend a lot of time in supermarkets, as well as other venues—from picturesque farmers' markets to the food aisles of chain drug stores—that sell food. One thing is certain—every other customer I talk to is as interested as you are and I am to eat better on a limited food budget. Those are the strategies you'll learn in this chapter.

Think of plotting and planning your supermarket trips as if you were planning to take the kids on a vacation. Your first step is to decide on your destination—what supermarket or other stores you'll use. After that you buy some guidebooks (in this case the Sunday newspaper) and do other research online (like print out coupons), and then you start looking for the good deals to get you to where you want to go.

In this case, where you want to go is to treat yourself to a vacation, and the way you're going to afford it in these challenging economic times is by savvy shopping. At any given moment there are *billions* of dollars of grocery coupons in the world waiting to be redeemed. If you spend a few cents on a stamp, it could reap many dollars coming back from manufacturers, and when you're eating food produced locally and seasonally, you're eating healthier, too.

In fact, in one week of following the tips in this chapter you will have more than made up for the cost of this book—and then you'll have all the cost-busting recipes to pamper your palate for years to come.

Most of the tips are specific to food shopping; this *is* a cookbook. But there are also hints for saving money in other segments of your budget. It's all coming out of the same wallet.

I wish I could promise you a clear and uncluttered path. But every rule has an exception, as you'll see below. What you're now doing is turning shopping from a simple ritual to a complex task. But the results are worth the effort you'll be putting in.

PLAN *BEFORE* YOU SHOP

The most important step to cost-effective cooking is to decide logically and intelligently what you're going to cook for the week. That may sound simple, but if you're in the habit of deciding when you're leaving work at the end of the day, chances are you've ended up with a lot of frozen pizza or Chinese carry-out.

The first step is to "shop" in a place you know well; it's your own kitchen. Look and see what's still in the refrigerator, and how that food—which you've already purchased and perhaps also cooked—can be utilized. That's where many recipes in this book come into play. Some leftover cooked carrots? Just check the recipes in this book and see all the ways they could be put to use.

Now look and see what foods you have in the freezer. Part of savvy shopping is stocking up on foods when they're on sale; in fact, sales of free-standing freezers have grown by more than 10 percent during the past few years, while sales of all other major appliances have gone down. And there's a good reason: A free-standing freezer allows you to take advantage of sales, especially on foods like boneless, skinless chicken breasts—the time-crunched cook's best friend—that go on sale frequently and are almost prohibitive in price when they're not on sale.

But preparing food for the freezer to insure its future quality is important. Never freeze meats, poultry, or seafood in the supermarket wrapping alone. To guard against freezer burn, double wrap food in freezer paper or place it in a heavy resealable plastic bag. Mark the purchase date on raw food, and the date the food was frozen on cooked items, and use them within three months.

Most supermarkets have a lower cost for buying larger quantities, and by freezing part of a package, you can take advantage of that savings. Scan recipes and look at the amount of the particular meat specified; that's what size your packages destined for the freezer should be.

A good investment is a kitchen scale to weigh portions, if you don't feel comfortable judging weight freestyle.

Keep a list taped to the front of your freezer. It should list the contents and date when each item was frozen. Mark off foods as you take them out and add foods as you put them in.

Also, part of your strategy is to actually cook only a few nights a week or on one day of a weekend; that means when you're making recipes that can be doubled—like soups and stews—you make larger batches and freeze a portion. Those meals are "dinner insurance" for nights you don't want to cook. Those are the nights that you previously would have brought in the bucket of chicken or the high-priced rotisserie chicken and spent far more money.

The other factor that enters into the initial planning is looking at your depletion list to see what foods and other products need to be purchased. A jar of peanut butter or a bottle of dishwashing liquid might not factor into meal plans, but they do cost money—so they have to be factored into your budget. Some weeks you might not need many supplies, but it always seems to me that all of the cleaning supplies seem to deplete the same week.

Now you've got the "raw data" to look at the weekly sales circulars from your newspaper or delivered with your mail. Those sales, along with online research to accrue even more money-saving coupons, should form the core for your menu planning.

COUPON CLIPPING 101

It's part art, it's part science, and it all leads to more money in your wallet. Consider this portion of the chapter your Guerilla Guide to Coupons. There's more to it than just clipping them. Of course, unless you clip them or glean them from other channels (see some ideas below), then you can't save money. So that's where you're going to start—but, trust me, it's just the beginning.

Forget that image you have of the lady wearing the hairnet and the "sensible shoes" in line at the supermarket digging through what seems to be a bottomless pit of tiny pieces of paper looking for the right coupon for this or that. Clipping coupons—in case you haven't heard—is *cool.*

And it should be, given the rewards. At any point in time there are *billions of dollars* of coupons floating around out there, according to the folks at www.grocerycouponguide.com, one of the growing list of similar sites dedicated to helping you save money.

Not only is it becoming easier to access these savings, you're a Neanderthal if you don't. The fact that you're reading this book—and will be cooking from it—shows that you care about trimming the size of your grocery bill. So it's time to get with the program.

Coupon usage grew by a whopping 192 percent in the year between March 2008 and March 2009, according to Coupons.com, which has seen an increase in traffic to its site of 25 percent per month since the current recession began.

Even the Sunday newspaper (as long as it still exists) is a treasure-trove of coupons. I found a $5 off coupon for a premium cat food my finicky cats liked in a local paper, which cost 50 cents. It was worth it to buy four copies of the paper; I spent $2, but I then netted an $18 savings on the cat food.

The Internet is increasingly a place to look for coupons, both for a few dollars here and there on groceries and for many dollars off on major purchases like computers or televisions. Stores like Target frequently have coupons for up to 10 percent off an order, too.

Here are some good sites to browse. For many coupons you have to download some free software to print them off; it's worth the few minutes of your time:

- www.GroceryCoupons.com

- www.CouponMom.com

- www.GroceryGuide.com

- www.PPGazette.com

- www.GroceryCoupons4U.com

LEARN THE LINGO
Coupons are printed on very small pieces of paper, and even with 20/20 eyesight or reading glasses many people—including me—need to use a magnifying glass to read all the fine print. There are many legal phrases that have to be part of every coupon, too.

In the same way that baseball fans know that RBI means "runs batted in," coupon collectors know that WSL means "while supplies last." Here's a list of many abbreviations found on coupons:

- **AR.** After rebate.

- **B1G1 or BOGO.** Buy one, get one free.

- **CRT.** Cash register receipt.

- **DC.** Double coupon, which is a coupon the store—not the manufacturer—doubles in value.

- **DCRT.** Dated cash register receipt, which proves you purchased the item during the right time period.

- **FAR.** Free after rebate.

- **IP.** Internet printed coupons.

- **ISO.** In-store only.

- **IVC.** Instant value coupon, which are the pull offs found on products in the supermarket that are redeemed as you pay.

- **MIR.** Mail-in rebate.

- **NED.** No expiration date.

- **OAS.** On any size, which means the coupon is good for any size package of that particular product.

- **OYNSO.** On your next shopping order, which means that you must return to the same store; the coupon will not be good at another store.

- **POP.** Proof of purchase, which are the little panels found on packages that you have to cut off and send in to receive a rebate.

- **WSL.** While supplies last, which means you can't demand a "rain check" to use the coupon at a later date once the product is once again in stock.

While you may be just becoming more aware of them, coupons are nothing new. They began in the late 1800s when Coca-Cola and Grape Nuts offered coupons to consumers. Currently more than 3,000 companies use coupons as part of their marketing plans, and shoppers save more than $5 billion a year by redeeming the coupons.

GET ORGANIZED!

So you now have a fistful of coupons with which you're going to save money at the supermarket. That's a start; if you don't have the coupons, you can't use them.

The first decision you have to make is how you're going to organize your coupons. There are myriad ways, and each has its fans. It's up to you to decide which is right for you, your family, and the way you shop:

- Arrange the coupons by aisle in the supermarket. This is only good if you shop in one store consistently.

- Arrange the coupons by category of product. Dairy products, cleaning supplies, paper disposables, and cereals are all categories with many weekly coupons, so arrange your coupons in this manner.

- Arrange the coupons alphabetically. This system works well if you redeem coupons in various types of stores beyond the grocery store.

- Arrange the coupons by expiration date. Coupons are only valid for a certain time period; it can be a few weeks or a few months. And part of the strategy of coupon clipping is to maximize the value, which frequently comes close to the expiration date. Some of the best coupons are those for "buy one, get one free." However, when the coupon first appears, the item is at full price. But what about two weeks later, when the item is on sale at your store? Then the "buy one, get one free" can mean you're actually getting four cans for the price of one at the original retail price.

Storage systems for arranging coupons are as varied as methods of organizing them. I personally use envelopes and keep the stack held together with a low-tech paper clip. I've also seen people with whole wallets and tiny accordion binders dedicated to coupons. If you don't have a small child riding on the top of the cart, another alternative is to get a loose-leaf notebook with clear envelopes instead of pages.

> Sometimes coupons expire *before* their stated expiration date because retailers allot so many dollars per promotion. If, for example, a retailer is offering a free widget if you buy a widget holder, and the widgets run out, there's probably a way to justify turning you away. Read the fine print.

BARGAIN SHOPPING 2.0

Every grocery store has weekly sales, and those foods are the place to start your planning for new purchases; that's how you're saving money beyond using coupons. And almost every town has competing super-market chains that offer different products on sale. It's worth your time to shop in a few venues, because it will generate the most savings. That way you can also determine which chain offers the best store brands and purchase them while you're there for the weekly bargains. Here are other ways to save:

- **Shuffle those cards.** Even if I can't convince you to clip coupons, the least you can do for yourself to save money is take the five minutes required to sign up for store loyalty cards; many national brands as well as store brands are on sale only when using the card. While the current system has you hand the card to the cashier at the checkout, that will be changing in the near future. Shopping carts will be equipped with card readers that will gen-erate instant coupons according to your purchasing habits. I keep my stack of loyalty cards in the glove box of my car; that way they don't clutter my purse, but I always have them when shopping.

- **Segregate items not on your list.** Some of these might be marked down meats or vegetables, and some might be impulse buys that end up in the cart despite your pledge to keep to the list. Place these items in the "baby rack" rather than in the cart; you'll have a good visual sense of how much money is represented.

- **"Junk mail" may contain more than junk.** Don't toss those Val-pak and other coupon envelopes that arrive in the mail. Look through them carefully, and you'll find not only coupons for food products, but for many services, too.

- **Look for blanket discounts.** While it does take time to cull coupons, many supermarket chains send flyers in the mail that offer a set amount off the total, for example $10 off a total of $50. These are the easiest way to save money, and many national drug store chains, such as CVS, do the same. Just remember to have a loyalty card for those stores to take advantage of the savings.

- **Spend a stamp to get a rebate.** Despite the current cost of a first-class postage stamp, sending in for rebates is still worth your trouble. Many large manufacturers are now sending out coupon books or cash vouchers usable in many stores to customers who mail in receipts demonstrating that they have purchased about $50 of products. For example, Procter & Gamble, the country's largest advertiser and the company for which the term "soap opera" was invented, is switching millions of dollars from the airwaves to these sorts of promotions.

- **Find bargains online.** There are the specific coupon sites listed on page 4, but there are other places to look, too. Go to specific manufacturers of foods you like, even high-end organic foods. You'll find coupons as well as redemption offers. I also look for the coupon offers on such culinary sites as www.epicurious.com and www.foodnetwork.com. You will find coupons there, some tied to actual recipes.

- **Find coupons in the store.** Look for those little machines projecting out from the shelves; they usually contain coupons that can be used instantly when you check out. Also, don't throw out your receipt until you've looked at it carefully. There are frequently coupons printed on the back. The cashier may also hand you other small slips of paper with your cash register receipt; most of them are coupons for future purchases of items you just bought. They may be from the same brand or they may be from a competing brand. Either way, they offer savings.

- **Stock up on cans.** Even if you live in a small apartment without a basement storage unit, it makes sense to stock up on canned goods when they're on sale. The answer is to use every spare inch of space. The same plastic containers that fit under your bed to hold out-of-season clothing can also become a pantry for canned goods.

- **Get a bargain buddy.** There's no question that supermarkets try to lure customers with "buy one, get one free" promotions, and sometimes one is all you really want. And those massive cases of paper towels at the warehouse clubs are also a good deal—if you have unlimited storage space. The answer? Find a bargain buddy with whom you can split large purchases. My friends and I also swap coupons we won't use but the other person will. Going back to my example of the cat food savings, there were dog food coupons on the same page, so I turned them over to a canine-owning friend.

PUSHING THE CART WITH PURPOSE

So it's a "new you" entering the supermarket. First of all, you have a list, and it's for more than a few days. And you're going to buy what's on your list. Here's the first rule: stick to that list. Never go shopping when you're hungry; that's when non-essential treats wind up in your basket.

Always go shopping alone; unwanted items end up in the cart to keep peace in the family. And—here's an idea that might seem counter-intuitive—go shopping when you're in a hurry. It's those occasions when you have the time to dawdle that the shortcakes end up coming home when all you really wanted were the strawberries.

But, as promised, here are some exceptions to the rule of keeping to your list. You've got to be flexible enough to take advantage of some unexpected, great sales. Next to frugality, flexibility is the key to saving money on groceries.

It's easy if the sale is a markdown on meat; you see the $2 off coupon and put it in the cart, with the intention of either cooking it that night or freezing it. All supermarkets mark down meat on the day before the expiration sticker. The meat is still perfectly fine, and should it turn out not to be, you can take it back for a refund. So go ahead and take advantage of the markdown.

Then you notice a small oval sticker with the word *Save*. Is turkey breast at $1.09 a real bargain? You'll know it is if you keep track of prices, and know that a few weeks ago it was $3.99 per pound.

You now have two options. Buy the off-list bargains and freeze them, or use them this week. In place of what? And what effect will that have on the rest of your list?

That's why I suggest freezing bargains, assuming you can absorb the extra cost on this week's grocery bill. If not, then look at what produce, shelf-stable, and dairy items on the list were tied to a protein you're now crossing off, and delete them too.

But meat isn't the only department of the supermarket that has "remainder bins." Look in produce, bakery, and grocery. I've gotten some perfectly ripe bananas with black spots—just the way they should be—for pennies a pound, while the ones that are bright yellow (and still tasteless) are five times the cost.

Almost all supermarkets are designed to funnel traffic first into the produce section; that is actually the last place you want to shop. Begin with the proteins, since many items in other sections of your list relate to the entrees of the dinners you have planned. Once they are gathered, go through and get the shelf-stable items, then the dairy products (so they will not be in the cart for too long), and end with the produce. Using this method, the fragile produce is on the top of the basket, not crushed by the gallons of milk.

The last step is packing the groceries. If you live in an area where you have the option of packing them yourself, place items stored together in the same bag. That way all of your produce can go directly into the refrigerator, and canned goods destined for the basement will be stored in one trip.

LEARNING THE ROPES

The well-informed shopper is the shopper who is saving money, and the information you need to make the best purchasing decision is right there on the supermarket shelves. It's the shelf tag that gives you the cost per unit of measurement. The units can be quarts for salad dressing, ounces for dry cereal, or pounds for canned goods. All you have to do is look carefully.

But you do have to make sure you're comparing apples to apples and oranges to oranges—or in this example, stocks to stocks. Some can be priced by the quart, while others are by the pound.

- **Check out store brands.** Store brands and generics have been improving in quality during the past few years, and according to *Consumer Reports,* buying them can save anywhere from 15 percent to 50 percent. Moving from a national brand to a store brand is a personal decision, and sometimes money is not the only factor. For example, I have used many store brands of chlorine bleach, and have returned to Clorox time and again. But I find no difference between generic corn flakes and those from the market leaders. Store brands can also be less expensive than national brands on sale—and with coupons.

- **Compare prices within the store.** Many foods—such as cold cuts and cheeses—are sold in multiple areas of the store, so check out those alternate locations. Sliced ham may be less expensive in a cellophane package shelved with the refrigerated foods than at the deli counter unless a brand is on sale.

- **Look for the bargain bins.** It's not just the meat department that marks down food; the produce and bakery departments do as well. Learn where these areas are in your supermarket, and hunt them regularly. For making breadcrumbs or croutons, it's even better to buy the slightly stale bread that's half price.

- **Look high and low.** Manufacturers pay a premium price to shelve products at eye level, and you're paying for that placement when you're paying their prices. Look at the top and bottom shelves in aisles like cereal and canned goods. That's where you'll find the lower prices.

- **Buy the basics.** When is a bargain not a bargain? When you're paying for water or you're paying for a little labor. That's why even though a 15-ounce can of beans is less expensive than the same quantity of dried beans (approximately a pound), you're still better off buying the dried beans. One pound of dried beans makes the equivalent of four or five cans of beans. In the same way, a bar of Monterey Jack cheese is much less expensive per pound than a bag of grated Monterey Jack cheese. In addition to saving money, the freshly grated cheese will have more flavor because cheese loses flavor rapidly when grated. And pre-cut and pre-washed vegetables are truly exorbitant.

- **Watch the scanner.** I know it's tempting to catch up on pop culture by leafing through the tabloids at the checkout, but that's the last thing you should be doing—and that's another reason to go shopping without the kids, because they will be a distraction. Watching the clerk scan your order usually saves you money. For example, make sure all the instant savings coupons are peeled off; this includes marked-down meats and coupons on boxes and bags. Then, make sure sale items are ringing up at the right price.

WASTE NOT, WANT NOT

We're now going to start listing exceptions to all the rules you just read, because a bargain isn't a bargain if you end up throwing some of it away. Remember that the goal is to waste nothing. Start by annotating your shopping list with quantities for the recipes you'll be cooking. That way you can begin to gauge when a bargain is a bargain. Here are other ways to buy only what you need:

- **Don't overbuy.** Sure, the large can of diced tomatoes is less per pound than the smaller can. But what will you do with the remainder of the can if all you need is a small amount? The same is true for dairy products. A half-pint of heavy cream always costs much more per ounce than a quart, but if the remaining 3 cups of cream will end up in the sink in a few weeks, go with the smaller size.

- **Buy what you'll eat, not what you *should* eat.** Ah, this is where parental guilt comes into play. You've just read an article on the wonders of broccoli, and there it is on sale. But if your family hates broccoli, the low sale cost doesn't matter; you'll end up throwing it away. We all think about healthful eating when we're in the supermarket, but if you know that the contents of your cart are good thoughts rather than realistic choices, you're wasting money.

- **Buy smart.** Just because you have a coupon doesn't mean you should buy something. We all love bargains, but if you're putting an item into your cart for the first time, you must decide if it's because you really want it and haven't bought it before because of its cost, or because you're getting $1.50 off of the price. This is a subset of buying what you eat, and not what you should eat.

- **Sometimes bigger isn't better.** If you're shopping for snacks for your kids, look for the *small* apples rather than the giant ones. Most kids take a few bites and then toss the rest, so evaluate any purchases you're making by the pound.

- **Ring that bell!** You know the one; it's always in the meat department of the supermarket. It might take you a few extra minutes, but ask the real live human who will appear for *exactly* what you want; many of the recipes in *$3 Meals Your Kids Will Love* specify less than the weight of packages you find in the meat case. Many supermarkets do not have personnel readily available in departments like the cheese counter, but if there are wedges of cheeses labeled and priced, then someone is in charge. It might be the deli department or the produce department, but find out who it is and ask for a small wedge of cheese if you can't find one that's cut to the correct size.

- **Check out the bulk bins.** Begin buying from the bulk bins for shelf-stable items, like various types of rice, beans, dried fruits, and nuts. Each of these departments has scales so you can weigh ingredients like dried mushrooms or pasta. If a recipe calls for a quantity rather than a weight, you can usually "eyeball" the quantity. If you're unsure of amounts, start by bringing a 1-cup measuring cup with you to the market. Empty the contents of the bin into the measuring cup rather than directly into the bag. One problem with bulk food bags is that they are difficult to store in the pantry; shelves were made for sturdier materials. Wash out plastic deli containers or even plastic containers that you bought containing yogurt or salsa. Use those for storage once the bulk bags arrive in the kitchen. Make sure you label your containers of bulk foods both at the supermarket and if you're transferring the foods to other containers at home so you know what they are, especially if you're buying similar foods. Arborio and basmati rice look very similar in a plastic bag, but they are totally different grains and shouldn't be substituted for each other.

- **Shop from the salad bar for tiny quantities.** There's no question that supermarkets charge a premium price for items in those chilled bins in the salad bar, but you get exactly what you need. When to shop there depends on the cost of the item in a larger quantity. At $4 per pound, you're still better off buying a 50-cent can of garbanzo beans, even if it means throwing some of them away. However, if you don't see how you're going to finish the $4 pint of cherry tomatoes, then spend $1 at the salad bar for the handful you need to garnish a salad.

SUPERMARKET ALTERNATIVES

All of the hints thus far in this chapter have been geared to pushing a cart around a supermarket. Here are some other ways to save money:

- **Shop at farmers' markets.** I admit it; I need a 12-step program to help me cure my addiction to local farmers' markets. Shopping alfresco on warm summer days turns picking out fruits and vegetables into a truly sensual experience. Also, you buy only what you want. There are no bunches of carrots; there are individual carrots sold by the pound. The U.S. Department of Agriculture began publishing the *National Directory of Farmers' Markets* in 1994, and at that time the number was fewer than 2,000. That figure has now doubled. To find a farmers' market near you, go to www.ams.usda.gov/farmersmarkets. The first cousins of farmers' markets for small quantities of fruits are the sidewalk vendors in many cities. One great advantage to buying from them is that their fruit is always ripe and ready to eat or cook.

- **Shop at ethnic markets.** If you live in a rural area this may not be possible, but even moderately small cities have a range of ethnic markets, and that's where you should buy ingredients to cook those cuisines. All the Asian condiments used in *$3 Meals Your Kids Will Love* are far less expensive at Asian markets than in the Asian aisle of your supermarket, and you can frequently find imported authentic brands instead of domestic versions; the same is true of Hispanic markets for ingredients such as green chiles and chipotle chiles. Even small cities and many towns have ethnic enclaves, such as a "Little Italy"; each neighborhood has some grocery stores with great prices for those ingredients and the fresh produce used to make the dishes, too.

- **Shop alternative stores.** Groceries aren't only at grocery stores; many "dollar stores" and other discount venues stock shelf-stable items. If you live in New England, Ocean State Job Lot should be on your weekly circuit; this discount store chain is loaded with food bargains.

- **Shop for food in drug stores.** Every national brand of drug-store—including CVS and Walgreen's—carries grocery products, and usually has great bargains each week. In the same way that food markets now carry much more than foods, drug stores stock thousands of items that have no connection to medicine. Those chains also have circulars in Sunday newspapers, so check them out—even if you're feeling very healthy.

- **Shop online.** In recent years it's become possible to do all your grocery shopping online through such services as Peapod and Fresh Direct. While there is frequently a delivery charge involved, for housebound people this is a true boon. If you really hate the thought of pushing the cart, you should explore it; it's impossible to make impulse buys. There are also a large number of online retailers for ethnic foods, dried herbs and spices, premium baking chocolate, and other shelf-stable items. Letting your cursor do the shopping for these items saves you time, and many of them offer free shipping at certain times of the year.

TIME FOR MENTAL CALISTHENICS

Just as an athlete goes through mental preparation before a big game, getting yourself "psyched" to save money is the first step to accomplishing that goal. You've got to get into a frugal frame of mind. You're out to save money on your food budget, but not feel deprived. You're going to be eating the delicious dishes in this book.

Think about where your food budget goes other than the grocery store. The cost of a few "designer coffee" treats at the local coffee shop is equal to a few dinners at home. Couldn't you brew coffee and take it to work rather than spend $10 a week at the coffee cart? And those cans of soft drinks in the vending machine are four times the cost of bringing a can from home. But do you really need soft drinks at all? For mere pennies you can brew a few quarts of ice tea, which has delicious flavor without chemicals.

Planning ahead is important, too. Rather than springing for a chilled bottle of spring water because you're thirsty in the supermarket, keep a few empty plastic bottles in your car and fill one from the water fountain. That water is free.

Until frugality comes naturally, do what diet counselors suggest, and keep a log of every penny spent of food. Just as the empty calories add up, so do the meaningless noshes.

Think about all those lunches you pay for—both for your kids and yourself. School lunches have increasingly been criticized for their lack of nutritional value, or your kids might be buying junk from vending machines if they still exist. So pack a delicious lunch, and avoid both pitfalls of "school food."

Packing lunches should become part of your routine, too. Bringing your lunch to work does increase your weekly supermarket tab, but it accomplishes a few good goals. It adds funds to the bottom line of your total budget, and it allows you to control what you're eating—and when.

If you have a pressured job, chances are there are days that you end up eating from snack food vending machines or eating fast food at your desk. If you bring your lunch you know what it will be—even if you don't know when you'll be eating it.

Almost every office has both a refrigerator and a microwave oven, so lunch can frequently be a leftover from a dinner the night or two before, so the extra cost and cooking time are minimal.

Frugality also extends to saving your old bags, if you shop at a store that gives you 5 cents off your order for each of your own bags you use. While 5 cents doesn't seem like much, it does add up. And you're helping the environment, too, because less packaging is ending up in landfills; the environmental term for it is "source reduction."

So now that you're becoming a grocery guru, you can move on to find myriad ways to save money on your grocery bill while eating wonderfully. That's what *$3 Meals Your Kids Will Love,* and the other books in the $3 Meals series, is all about.

Chapter 2:
Cooking Healthy Meals for Happy Kids

Saving lots of money while investing just a small amount of your time is one of the underpinnings of all $3 Meals books. Those are the tricks you'll learn in this chapter.

You'll learn how to cut up various types of meat, and how to select fish. You'll also get a bit of "homework" at the end of the chapter. While there are hundreds of recipes in *$3 Meals Your Kids Will Love* that are on the table in less time than it takes them to watch their favorite cartoon show, some of these depend on the availability of precooked poultry and ham. Those foods are exorbitantly high-priced if you buy them at the supermarket, so cook them yourself and keep them in the freezer always. They are foods that go on sale frequently, too.

The chapter ends with a few other basic recipes that are like a slow leak in your grocery budget. Once you learn to make your own bread-crumbs and tomato sauce, there's more to spend elsewhere.

PROCEDURES FOR POULTRY

Just look at the range of prices for chicken in the supermarket! They can range from less than $1 per pound for whole birds and leg/thigh quarters to $5 or $6 per pound for coveted boneless, skinless breasts. Always keep in mind that you're paying for someone else's labor, and that's money you can "make" yourself.

It is far more economical to purchase a whole chicken and cut it up yourself, rather than to buy one already cut. There are also times that your choice of chicken pieces isn't available, and you can always cut up a few chickens to glean the parts for that meal, and freeze what's left; another benefit is that you can save the scraps and freeze them to keep you "stocked up" for soups and sauces. Here are some methods of chicken cutting you should know:

- **Cutting up a whole chicken:** Start by breaking back the wings until the joints snap, then use a boning knife to cut through the ball joints and detach the wings. When holding the chicken on its side, you will see a natural curve outlining the boundary between the breast and the leg/thigh quarters. Use sharp kitchen shears and cut along this line. Cut the breast in half by scraping away the meat from the breastbone, and using a small paring knife to remove the wishbone. Cut away the breastbone using the shears, and save it for stock. Divide the leg/thigh quarters by turning the pieces over and finding the joint joining them. Cut through the joint and sever the leg from the thigh.

- **Boning chicken breasts:** If possible, buy the chicken breasts whole rather than split. Pull the skin off with your fingers, and then make an incision on either side of the breastbone, cutting down until you feel the bone resisting the knife. Treating one side at a time, place the blade of your boning knife against the carcass, and scrape away the meat. You will then have two pieces—the large fillet and the small tenderloin. To trim the fillet, cut away any fat. Some recipes will tell you to pound the breast to an even thickness, so it will cook evenly and quickly. Place the breast between two sheets of plastic wrap or waxed paper, and pound with the smooth side of a meat mallet or the bottom of a small, heavy skillet or saucepan. If you have a favorite veal scallop recipe, and want to substitute chicken or turkey, pound it very thin—to a thickness of 1/4 inch. Otherwise, what you are after is to pound the thicker portion so that it lays and cooks evenly. To trim the tenderloin, secure the tip of the tendon that will be visible with your free hand. Using a paring knife, scrape down the tendon, and the meat will push away.

HANDLING POULTRY

Poultry should always be rinsed under cold running water after being taken out of the package. If it's going to be pre-browned in the oven or in a skillet on the stove, pat the pieces dry with paper towels and then wash your hands. Chicken often contains salmonella, a naturally occurring bacteria that is killed by cooking, but you don't want to transfer this bacteria to other foods.

While rules have been changing for pork in the past few years, chicken still must be cooked to an internal temperature of 165°F to ensure that there's no chance for microorganisms to survive. The best way to test the temperature is to use an instant-read meat thermometer.

When the thickest part of the chicken is probed, the reading should be 165°F. But if you don't want to take the temperature of every piece of chicken, here are the visual signals: The chicken is tender when poked with the tip of a paring knife, there is not a hint of pink even near the bones, and the juices run clear. Always test the dark meat before the white meat. Dark meat takes slightly longer to cook, so if the thighs are the proper temperature, you know the breasts will be fine.

HERE'S THE BEEF

The best beef, in terms of both flavor and texture, comes from cows 18 to 24 months old. Beef is graded in the United States by the Department of Agriculture as Prime, Choice, or Select. Prime is usually reserved for restaurants, and the other two are found in supermarkets. Since the age, color, texture, and marbling are what determine its category, Prime beef is the most marbled and contains the most fat.

When you're looking at beef in the case, seek deep red, moist meat generously marbled with white fat. Yellow fat is a tip-off to old age. Beef is purple after cutting, but the meat quickly "blooms" to bright red on exposure to the air. Well-aged beef is dark and dry. To avoid paying for waste, be sure meat is thoroughly trimmed by a butcher. Otherwise a low per-pound price can translate into a higher cost for the edible portion.

You can usually save money by cutting the meat into cubes your-self. The general guideline is that if it's less expensive, then it's the cut you want, but here are some specifics:

- Chuck is the beef taken from between the neck and shoulder blades. Some chuck roasts also contain a piece of the blade bone, but it's easy to cull the meat from a chuck roast.

- Round is the general name for the large quantity of beef from the hind leg extending from the rump to the ankle. The eye of the round and the bottom round are the two least tender cuts, while the top round should be reserved for roasting.

PORKY PARTS

Pork has very little internal connective tissue and is inherently tender, because pigs don't wander and run around the prairies like cows and lambs. It is one of the few meats that can be equally good roasted or slowly braised in aromatic liquid. With the exception of pork shoulder, which is more muscular and fatty and should be cooked with liquid, almost all loin cuts can be done either way.

Pork has layers of fat that encircle the meat rather than marbling it. Some fat should be left on so that the meat does not dry out when cooking.

With the exception of the tenderloin, which will become stringy if subjected to long, slow cooking, almost all cuts of pork are up for grabs. That's why you don't find pre-cut pork for stews the way that other animals' trimmings are packaged. Just choose pork that looks lean and is the least expensive.

The two best cuts of pork for soups and stews are boneless country ribs and boneless loin. Very often whole loins—usually about 10 pounds—are on sale for a very low price, so it is worth it to buy one and freeze most for future meals. Boneless country ribs, on the other hand, are the pork equivalent of a chuck roast; they have great flavor and become meltingly tender.

One warning regarding spare ribs is in order. While they're great on the grill, use only the boneless country ribs for braised dishes, because the percentage of bone to meat is so great that ribs require far too much liquid to cook.

CREATIVE CUTTING

Compared to the precision needed to cut a whole chicken into its component parts, boning and cutting beef or pork is a free-for-all. The bones should be removed, however. Not only do they take up space needed for vegetables in your Dutch oven, but the bones slow down the cooking process, too, because they absorb heat and take it away from the meat. But do save any beef bones for making Beef Stock (recipe on page 56); unfortunately pork bones do not make a good stock. But another great stock can be made with a big ham bone; follow the recipe for Beef Stock.

The first step of boning is to cut away the bones. Then cut away any large areas of fat that can be easily discarded. The last step is to decide how the remaining boneless meat should be cut. Read your recipe to determine how large the cubes should be.

The rule is to cut across the grain rather than with the grain. If you're not sure which way the grain runs, make a test slice. You should see the ends of fibers if you cut across the grain. The reason for this is that meat becomes more tender if the ends of the fibers are exposed to the liquid and heat.

PROCEDURAL PROWESS

The one major principle for almost all the recipes in this book is the initial browning of the meat, which means cooking the meat quickly over moderately high heat. This causes the surface of the food to brown. In the case of cubes of beef for stew, browning seals in the juices and keeps the interior moist; for ground meats, browning gives food an appetizing color, allows you to drain off some of the inherent fat, and also gives dishes a rich flavor.

While larger pieces can be browned under an oven broiler, ground meats are browned in a skillet. Crumble the meat in a skillet over medium-high heat. Break up the lumps with a meat fork or the back of a spoon as it browns, and then stir it around frequently until all lumps are brown and no pink remains. At that point, it's easy to remove it from the pan with a slotted spoon, and discard the grease from the pan. You can then use the pan again without washing it for any pre-cooking of other ingredients.

CUTTING THE CALORIES

In addition to cost, another benefit of braising meats is that it's possible to remove a great percentage of the saturated fat. It's easy to find and discard this "bad fat," both before and after cooking.

On raw meat, you just look for it. It's the white stuff around the red stuff. Cut it off with a sharp paring knife, and you're done.

While some fat remains in the tissue, much of the saturated fat is released during the cooking process, and there are ways to discard it both hot and cold. We'll start with the easiest thing: If you're cooking in advance and refrigerating a dish, all the fat rises to the top and hardens once chilled. Just scrape it off and throw it away.

The same principle of fat rising to the surface is true when food is hot, but it's a bit harder to eliminate it. Tilt the pan, and the fat will form a puddle on the lower side. It's then easier to scoop it off with a soup ladle. When you're down to too little to scoop off, level the pan, and blot the top with paper towels. You'll get even more fat off with this process.

FISHY BUSINESS

While fish frequently costs more than most meats, there is no waste to a fish fillet, and with its low fat content it doesn't shrink the way that meats do. So the price per edible ounce of fish is really about the same as for other forms of protein like a chuck roast or pork loin, if still more expensive than a chicken. Fish are high in protein and low to moderate in fat, cholesterol, and sodium. A 3-ounce portion of fish has between 47 and 170 calories depending on the species. Fish is an excellent source of B vitamins, iodine, phosphorus, potassium, iron, and calcium.

The most important nutrient in fish may be the omega-3 fatty acids. These are the primary polyunsaturated fatty acids found in the fat and oils of fish. They have been found to lower the levels of low-density lipoproteins (LDL), the "bad" cholesterol, and raise the levels of high-density lipoproteins (HDL), the "good" cholesterol. Fatty fish that live in cold water, such as mackerel and salmon, seem to have the most omega-3 fatty acids, although all fish have some.

BOUNTIFUL OPTIONS

It's more important to use the freshest fish—and one that is reasonably priced—than any specific fish; that's why these recipes are not written for cod, halibut, or pompano. They're written for two generic types of fish—thin white-fleshed fillets and thick white-fleshed fillets. These encompass most types of fish. They are all low in fat, mild to delicate in flavor, and flake easily when cooked.

The only species of fish that should *not* be used in these recipes are tuna, bluefish, and mackerel; they all will be too strong. Salmon, if you find it at a good price, can be substituted for either classification of fish, depending on the thickness of the fillet.

There are thousands of species that fit these rather large definitions. Here are some of the most common:

- **Thin fillets:** Flounder, sole, perch, red snapper, trout, tilapia, ocean perch, catfish, striped bass, turbot, and whitefish.

- **Thick fillets:** Halibut, scrod, grouper, sea bass, mahi-mahi, pompano, yellowtail, and swordfish.

SECRETS TO SELECTION

Most supermarkets still display fish on chipped ice in a case rather than pre-packaging it, and they should. Fish should be kept at an even lower temperature than meats. Fish fillets or steaks should look bright, lustrous, and moist, with no signs of discoloration or drying.

When making your fish selection, keep a few simple guidelines in mind. Above all, do not buy any fish that actually smells fishy, indicating that it is no longer fresh or hasn't been cut or stored properly. Fresh fish has the mild, clean scent of the sea—nothing more. Look for bright, shiny colors in the fish scales, because as a fish sits, its skin becomes more pale and dull looking. Then peer into the eyes; they should be black and beady. If they're milky or sunken, the fish has been dead too long. And if the fish isn't behind glass, gently poke its flesh. If the indentation remains, the fish is old.

Rinse all fish under cold running water before cutting or cooking. With fillets, run your fingers in every direction along the top of the fillet before cooking, and feel for any pesky little bones.

You can remove bones easily in two ways. Larger bones will come out if they're stroked with a vegetable peeler, and you can pull out smaller bones with tweezers. This is not a long process, but it's a gesture that will be greatly appreciated by all who eat the fish.

TALKING TUNA

There is a dizzying array of cans, and now pouches, on supermarket shelves, but they essentially fall into four categories. They are solid white tuna packed in water, solid white tuna packed in oil, and the same packing options for light tuna. Water-packed tuna is a relative newcomer to the market, following decades of oil-packed tuna. While it does trim the fat from the fish, it also trims much of the flavor since it tends to be less moist.

There are health concerns as well as cost reasons for specifying light tuna rather than white tuna, sometimes called albacore tuna, in these recipes. White tuna has been found to be much higher in mercury than light tuna, so light tuna is better on both scores. Feel free in any of the recipes containing canned tuna to substitute canned salmon. Almost all canned salmon is packaged complete with bones and skin, however, so some preparatory work is needed before using it in recipes.

COOKING WITH WINE AND BEER

It is true that not all the alcohol evaporates when you cook with wine or beer; however, what remains is extremely limited. For example, if a dish cooks for one hour, then 25 percent of the alcohol remains. But this is one-quarter of the 6 percent alcohol that was in the wine or beer at the beginning of the cooking time. If you use 1 cup of wine in cooking, then a whole batch of sauce would contain the same alcohol content as $\frac{1}{4}$ cup of wine.

Not a single member of the Parents Panel had any concern about serving his or her kids dishes that contain wine or beer. But if you do, there are options. There are now non-alcoholic versions of both wine and beer, and you can use these in cooking.

Basic Roast Chicken

Once you have a cache of cooked chicken in the freezer, there are literally hundreds of ways to have dinner on the table in a matter of minutes. If you make a large roasting chicken on a weekend day, you can serve the parts your family likes best fresh from the oven. Then freeze the rest in the size portions specified in most recipes, which is 2–3 cups.

Yield: 6–8 servings | **Active time:** 15 minutes | **Start to finish:** 2 hours

1 (5–7-pound) roasting chicken
4 sprigs fresh parsley, divided
4 sprigs fresh rosemary, divided
4 garlic cloves, peeled and minced, divided
2 sprigs fresh thyme or 2 teaspoons dried thyme
Salt and freshly ground black pepper to taste
4 tablespoons (½ stick) unsalted butter, softened
1 large onion, peeled and roughly chopped
1 carrot, peeled and thickly sliced
1 celery rib, rinsed, trimmed, and sliced
1 cup Chicken Stock (recipe on page 55) or purchased stock

1. Preheat the oven to 425°F. Rinse chicken, and pat dry with paper towels. Place 2 sprigs parsley, 2 sprigs rosemary, 2 garlic cloves, and thyme in cavity of chicken. Sprinkle salt and pepper inside cavity, and close it with skewers and string.

2. Chop remaining parsley, rosemary, and garlic. Mix with butter, and season to taste with salt and pepper. Gently stuff mixture under the skin of the breast meat. Rub skin with salt and pepper. Place chicken on a rack in a roasting pan, breast side up.

3. Bake for 30 minutes, then reduce the oven temperature to 350°F, and add onion, carrot, and celery to the roasting pan. Cook an additional 1–1½ hours, or until chicken is cooked through and no longer pink, and white meat registers 160°F and dark meat registers 165°F on an instant-read thermometer. Remove chicken from the oven, and allow it to rest on a heated platter for 10 minutes.

4. Spoon grease out of the pan, and add the chicken stock. Stir over medium-high heat until the liquid is reduced to a syrupy consistency. Strain sauce into a sauce boat, and add to it any liquid that accumulates on the platter when the chicken is carved. Serve immediately.

Note: The chicken can be roasted up to 3 hours in advance and kept at room temperature, covered with aluminum foil.

Variations:

- Use 3 tablespoons smoked Spanish paprika, 1 tablespoon ground cumin, 1 tablespoon dried thyme, and 3 minced garlic cloves.
- Use 3 tablespoons Italian seasoning, 3 tablespoons chopped fresh parsley, and 3 garlic cloves.
- Use 3 tablespoons dried oregano and 3 garlic cloves, and add 1 sliced lemon to the cavity.
- Rather than chicken stock, deglaze the pan with white wine.

Here's how to carve a roast chicken or turkey: To add a flourish to carving that also assures crisp skin for all, first "unwrap" the breast. Use a well-sharpened knife and fork. Carve and serve one side at a time. From the neck, cut just through the skin down middle of the breast and around the side. Hook the fork on the skin at the tail and roll the skin back to neck. Holding the bird with the fork, remove the leg by severing the hip joint. Separate the drumstick from the thigh and serve. Cut thin slices of the breast at a slight angle and add a small piece of rolled skin to each serving. Repeat all steps for the other side. Remove the wings last.

Basic Roast Turkey

There are two schools of thought to roasting a turkey—use either relatively low heat or high heat—and I prefer the latter. Using this roasting method, the turkey basically steams; the meat remains moist since it is now being cooked by a moist rather than dry heat method. You can use cooked turkey in any recipe calling for cooked chicken.

Yield: 8–10 servings, plus enough for leftovers | **Active time:** 15 minutes | **Start to finish:** at least 2¼ hours, but varies by the weight of the turkey

> 1 (12–16-pound) turkey
> 6 tablespoons (¾ stick) unsalted butter, softened and divided
> 3 garlic cloves, peeled and minced
> 3 tablespoons smoked Spanish paprika
> 1 tablespoon dried thyme
> Salt and freshly ground black pepper to taste
> 1 large onion, peeled and diced
> 1½ cups Chicken Stock (recipe on page 55) or purchased stock
> 1 tablespoon cornstarch
> 2 tablespoons cold water

1. Preheat the oven to 450°F. Rinse turkey inside and out under cold running water, and place it in a large roasting pan.
2. Combine 3 tablespoons butter, garlic, paprika, thyme, salt, and pepper in a small bowl, and mix well. Rub mixture over skin of turkey and inside cavity. Place onions and stock in the roasting pan, and place turkey on top of it. Create a tent with two sheets of heavy-duty aluminum foil, crimping foil around the edges of the roasting pan, and joining the two sheets in the center by crimping.
3. Place turkey in the oven, and roast for 12–15 minutes per pound. After 2 hours remove the foil, and remove liquid from the roasting pan with a bulb baster and reserve. Return turkey to the oven, covered as before.
4. Reduce the oven temperature to 350°F, and uncover turkey for the last 1 hour of roasting so skin browns. Rub skin with remaining butter after removing the foil. Turkey is done when it is cooked through and no longer pink, and dark meat registers 165°F on an instant-read thermometer. Remove turkey from the oven, and allow it to rest on a heated platter for 10–15 minutes, lightly covered with foil.

5. While turkey rests, prepare gravy. Pour all juices and flavoring ingredients from the roasting pan into a saucepan. If there are any brown bits clinging to the bottom of the pan, add back 1 cup of stock. Stir over medium heat, scraping brown bits from bottom of pan. In a small bowl, mix cornstarch and water, and set aside. Remove as much fat as possible from the surface of juices with a soup ladle, and then reduce liquid by at least ¼ to concentrate flavor. Stir cornstarch mixture into the pan, and cook for 3–5 minutes, or until liquid boils and slightly thickens. Season gravy to taste with salt and pepper.

6. To serve, carve turkey, and pass gravy separately.

Note: The turkey can be left at room temperature for up to 1 hour after removing it from the oven; keep it lightly tented with aluminum foil.

Variations:
- Use 2 tablespoons herbes de Provence or Italian seasoning along with 3 garlic cloves.
- Use ¼ cup chopped fresh rosemary, 1 tablespoon grated lemon zest, and 3 garlic cloves.

Basic Baked Ham

Not only does this recipe render the ham succulent and moist, it also creates some wonderful stock to use for your next batch of soup or a stew! This is a master recipe, and creates enough meat for a lavish Sunday dinner plus leftovers for myriad recipes located in other chapters of this book. Plus always save the ham bone for making soups.

Yield: 10–12 servings | **Active time:** 10 minutes | **Start to finish:** 2¾–3 hours

HAM

1 (8–10-pound) fully cooked ham (*not* spiral-sliced)
1½ cups Chicken Stock (recipe on page 55) or purchased stock
1 small onion, peeled and diced
1 small carrot, peeled and sliced
3 parsley sprigs

GLAZE (OPTIONAL)

½ cup apricot preserves
3 tablespoons grainy mustard
2 tablespoons grated fresh ginger

1. Preheat the oven to 325°F, and grease a large roasting pan.
2. Remove ham from plastic, if necessary, and rinse well under cold water. Cut away and discard any thick skin with a sharp knife, and trim all fat to an even ¼-inch layer.
3. Place ham, cut side down, in the prepared pan, and add stock, onion, carrot, and parsley. Cover the pan with heavy-duty aluminum foil, and bake ham for 1¾ hours. Remove ham from the oven, discard foil, and remove pan juices; save juices and freeze for soups and stews. Turn ham over, and bake for an additional 1–1½ hours, or until an instant-read thermometer registers 145°F.
4. While ham bakes, make glaze, if using. Combine apricot preserves, mustard, and ginger in a small mixing bowl, and stir well. Increase oven temperature to 400°F, if serving glazed ham. Remove ham from the oven. Cut off all ham to be used for future dishes, and apply glaze to remaining ham.

5. Return ham to the oven and bake for an additional 15 minutes, basting with glaze every 5 minutes.

Note: The ham can be prepared up to 3 days in advance and refrigerated, tightly covered. Serve it cold, or slice and reheat it in a 350°F oven for 5–10 minutes, or until warm.

Variations:
- Substitute ³/₄ cup dry sherry or white wine for ³/₄ cup of stock.
- Substitute ¹/₂ cup orange marmalade or red currant jelly for the apricot preserves.
- Glaze alternative: Reduce 3 cups of pineapple juice to ³/₄ cup, and add ¹/₄ cup Dijon mustard, ¹/₄ cup firmly packed dark brown sugar, and ¹/₄ teaspoon ground cloves.
- Glaze alternative: Substitute the same amount of prepared horseradish for the mustard.

I have no idea why spiral-sliced hams have become the norm rather than the exception; they are always more expensive than ham that is not sliced and it's nary impossible to cook one without having dried-out slices. Also, because the slices are so thin, you are severely limited as to the recipes you can make with the leftovers.

Herbed Tomato Sauce

This sauce is the "utility infielder" of my cooking; it plays a role in myriad dishes, and it contains lots of veggies your kids won't notice. You can also freeze the sauce for up to six months.

Yield: 2 cups | **Active time:** 15 minutes | **Start to finish:** 1 hour

 ¼ cup olive oil
 1 medium onion, peeled and finely chopped
 2 garlic cloves, peeled and minced
 1 carrot, peeled and finely chopped
 1 celery rib, rinsed, trimmed, and finely chopped
 1 (28-ounce) can crushed tomatoes, undrained
 2 tablespoons chopped fresh parsley
 2 teaspoons dried oregano
 1 teaspoon dried thyme
 2 bay leaves
 Salt and freshly ground black pepper to taste

1. Heat olive oil in 2-quart saucepan over medium heat. Add onion and garlic and cook, stirring frequently, for 3 minutes, or until onion is translucent.
2. Add carrot, celery, tomatoes, parsley, oregano, thyme, and bay leaves. Bring to a boil, reduce heat to low, and simmer the sauce uncovered, stirring occasionally, for 40 minutes, or until lightly thickened. Season to taste with salt and pepper.

Note: The sauce can be made up to 3 days in advance and refrigerated, tightly covered. Bring back to a simmer before serving.

Variation:
- If you do a lot of Hispanic cooking, substitute cilantro for the parsley and ground cumin for the thyme.

Basic White Sauce

White sauces form the base for a range of dishes, from creamed soups to macaroni and cheese and Italian lasagna. They are made with either milk or stock and thickened with a roux made by cooking butter with flour.

Yield: 2 cups | **Active time:** 15 minutes | **Start to finish:** 20 minutes

    3 tablespoons unsalted butter
    3 tablespoons all-purpose flour
    2 cups hot whole milk
    Salt and freshly ground black pepper to taste

1. Melt butter in a saucepan over low heat. Stir in flour, and cook, stirring constantly, for 2 minutes, or until mixture bubbles.
2. Slowly but steadily pour milk into the pan, whisking constantly, over medium heat until sauce comes to a boil. Simmer 2–3 minutes, thinning with more liquid if necessary to reach the right consistency. Season to taste with salt and pepper.

Note: The sauce can be made up to 3 days in advance and refrigerated, tightly covered. Reheat it over low heat, stirring occasionally, or in a microwave oven.

Variations:
- Add ³/₄ cup grated cheese (cheddar, smoked cheddar, Swiss, Gruyère) to the thickened sauce, and cook over low heat until the cheese melts.
- Add 2–3 tablespoons smooth or grainy Dijon mustard.
- Substitute ¹/₂ cup dry white wine for ¹/₂ cup of the milk, and add 3–4 tablespoons chopped fresh herbs.
- Substitute 1 cup chicken stock for 1 cup of milk; this will produce a lighter sauce.

If the sauce is lumpy, push it through a sieve, and then whisk it again to a simmer over low heat. Also, all white sauces form a skin as they cool. Push a sheet of plastic wrap directly into the surface of the sauce or whisk it as it cools to prevent this from happening.

Chapter 3:
Soup for Supper

Your kids love soup, and they know all about it. Maybe their first foray into soups came when you read them *Alice's Adventures in Wonderland.* Here's a testimonial to soups from that children's classic:

> *Beautiful soup, so rich and green*
> *Waiting in a hot tureen!*
> *Who for such dainties would not stoop?*
> *Soup of the evening, beautiful soup!*
> *Beautiful soup! Who cares for fish*
> *Game, or any other dish?*
> *Who would not give all else for two*
> *Pennyworth of beautiful soup?*

The soup recipes in this chapter are for times when soup is the meal. If you're serving one of these hearty soups before an entree, you can count on getting eight to twelve servings, depending on how generous you are with the portions.

In addition to being incredibly easy to make, soups are also open to endless substitutions and can become a great way to use the bits of this or that that collect in your refrigerator from other meals. Any plain steamed vegetable from a previous meal can be added into a soup, and the same is true for the half can of beans remaining from making chili con carne or the one piece of cooked chicken from a previous meal. Add cooked food to soups at the end of the cooking time, so that they don't get mushy and tasteless as part of the cooking process.

And make a double recipe of soups from time to time. The ones in this chapter all freeze extremely well, and can serve as your "dinner insurance" for a night in the future.

STOCKING UP

The four recipes for homemade stocks that you'll find in this chapter are some of the basic ways you can save money at the supermarket. You can't make a quart of milk at home unless you own a few cows, and you can't make a quart of orange juice unless you have some orange trees. But you can make a quart of stock—and it costs virtually pennies because you'll be using foods formerly destined for the garbage can or the compost bin. Recipes for soups and stews use a lot of stock, but this category of easily prepared food is found in almost all cooking.

It's the long-simmered homemade stocks that add the depth of flavor to the soups and sauces enjoyed at fine restaurants. Classically trained chefs have known for centuries what you're about to learn in this chapter—making stocks is as hard as boiling water and, if you're judicious and save bits and pieces destined for the garbage when prepping foods to be cooked, they're almost free.

Those onion and carrot peels, the bottoms of celery ribs, the stems from which you've stripped the leaves of fresh parsley—all are used to flavor stocks. If you take the time to bone your own chicken breasts or cut up your own beef stew meat from a roast—which I encourage you to do and tell you how to do in Chapter 2 of this book—then you have everything you need to make stock.

Perhaps you never considered commercial stocks—many of which are loaded with sodium—to be "convenience foods." But that's what they are, and you'll start to experience a significant savings when you begin making them yourself.

Cans and cartons of stocks are priced in many supermarkets in a way to confuse you; some are calculated by the pound, while others are by the ounce. Looking at a range of costs as well as flavors at a recent taste testing, a generic stock that tasted like salted water with some chemical chicken flavor was still a whopping $2 per quart, while one that actually had some flavor was almost $5 per quart.

Cheddar Potato Chowder

Cheesy potatoes are a food kids love, so they'll love this hearty chowder. Potatoes add a natural thickness and creaminess to this hearty chowder. Serve it with some crunchy coleslaw and cornbread.

Yield: 4–6 servings | **Active time:** 20 minutes | **Start to finish:** 50 minutes

  3 tablespoons unsalted butter
  1 medium onion, peeled and diced
  1 medium carrot, peeled and diced
  1 celery rib, rinsed, trimmed, and diced
  1 garlic clove, peeled and minced
  2 pounds redskin potatoes, scrubbed and diced
  4½ cups Vegetable Stock (recipe on page 57) or purchased stock
  1 teaspoon dried thyme
  1½ cups grated sharp cheddar cheese
  1 cup half-and-half
  Salt and freshly ground black pepper to taste
  3 tablespoons chopped fresh parsley

1. Heat butter in a 4-quart saucepan over medium-high heat. Add onion, carrot, celery, and garlic, and cook, stirring frequently, for 3 minutes, or until onion is translucent. Add potatoes, stock, and thyme, and stir well.
2. Bring to a boil, then reduce the heat to low and simmer soup, covered, for 25–30 minutes, or until vegetables are tender. Mash some of the vegetables with a potato masher until consistency you want is reached; the more that is mashed, the thicker the soup will be.
3. Add cheese and half-and-half, and cook for 5–10 minutes, or until cheese melts and soup simmers. Season to taste with salt and pepper, and ladle soup into bowls, sprinkling each serving with chopped parsley.

Note: The soup can be made up to 2 days in advance and refrigerated, tightly covered. Reheat it over low heat, covered.

Variations:

- For a Southwestern chowder, add 1 (4-ounce) can diced mild green chiles and 1 tablespoon ground cumin, and substitute cilantro for the parsley.
- Add 1 (10-ounce) package frozen corn, thawed, along with the half-and-half and cheese.
- Substitute Swiss cheese for the cheddar cheese, and add 1 (10-ounce) package frozen chopped spinach, thawed and drained well, along with the half-and-half and cheese.

Cheese should always be added at the end of the cooking time. Cheese has a tendency to scorch and/or curdle if added too early.

Southwestern Bean, Squash, and Corn Soup

Beans, squash, and corn are all crops that began in the Americas, and it was the Native Americans teaching European settlers how to grow them that assured the survival of settlements like Plymouth and Jamestown. This soup is from the Southwestern tradition.

Yield: 4–6 servings | **Active time:** 20 minutes | **Start to finish:** 55 minutes

    2 tablespoons olive oil
    1 medium onion, peeled and diced
    2 garlic cloves, peeled and minced
    1 small green bell pepper, seeds and ribs removed, and diced
    1 celery rib, rinsed, trimmed, and diced
    2 tablespoons chili powder
    1 teaspoon ground cumin
    1 teaspoon dried oregano
    4 cups Vegetable Stock (recipe on page 57) or purchased stock
    1 (1-pound) butternut squash, peeled and cut into 1-inch chunks
    1 (15-ounce) can kidney beans, drained and rinsed
    1 cup fresh corn kernels or frozen corn kernels, thawed
    Salt and freshly ground black pepper to taste

Adult additions:

    1–2 chipotle chiles in adobe sauce, finely chopped
    2–3 tablespoons chopped fresh cilantro

1. Heat olive oil in a 4-quart saucepan over medium-high heat. Add onion, garlic, green bell pepper, and celery. Cook, stirring frequently, for 3 minutes, or until onion is translucent. Add chili powder, cumin, and oregano, and cook for 1 minute, stirring constantly.

2. Add stock and squash, and bring to a boil over high heat, stirring occasionally. Reduce the heat to low, and simmer soup, covered, for 30 minutes, or until squash is almost tender.

3. Add beans and corn, and cook for 5–10 minutes, or until squash is very tender. Season to taste with salt and pepper, and serve immediately. Add chipotle chiles and cilantro to adult portions, if desired.

Note: The soup can be prepared up to 2 days in advance and refrigerated, tightly covered. Reheat it over low heat, covered, until hot, stirring occasionally.

Variation:

- Substitute acorn squash for the butternut squash, and pinto beans for the kidney beans.

If you can find peeled butternut squash in the supermarket, buy it. It's not a convenience food; it's a great time saver. It's more expensive per pound, but there are no seeds or peel to discard, so it's 100 percent edible.

Boston Baked Bean Soup

It's frequently easier to introduce kids to new foods if they're closely related to foods they already know and love, and that's the case with this soup. It's flavored just like the beans they love with hot dogs, but in a soup version.

Yield: 4–6 servings | **Active time:** 20 minutes | **Start to finish:** 3 hours, including 1 hour for beans to soak

1½ cups dry navy beans
3 tablespoons vegetable oil
1 large onion, peeled and diced
1 large carrot, peeled and diced
2 celery ribs, rinsed, trimmed, and diced
2 garlic cloves, peeled and minced
2 tablespoons smoked Spanish paprika
2 teaspoons chili powder
3 cups Vegetable Stock (recipe on page 57) or purchased stock
1 (28-ounce) can diced tomatoes, undrained
½ cup ketchup
¼ cup pure maple syrup
¼ cup cider vinegar
1 tablespoon Dijon mustard
Salt and freshly ground black pepper to taste

Adult additions:
Hot red pepper sauce to taste
Additional Dijon mustard to taste

1. Rinse beans in a colander and place them in a mixing bowl covered with cold water. Allow beans to soak overnight. Or place beans into a saucepan and bring to a boil over high heat. Boil 1 minute. Turn off the heat, cover the pan, and soak beans for 1 hour. With either soaking method, drain beans, discard soaking water, and begin cooking as soon as possible.

2. Heat oil in a 4-quart saucepan over medium-high heat. Add onion, carrot, celery, and garlic. Cook, stirring frequently, for 3 minutes, or until onion is translucent. Stir in paprika and chili powder, and cook for 1 minute, stirring constantly.

3. Add beans, stock, tomatoes, ketchup, maple syrup, vinegar, and mustard, and stir well. Bring to a boil over medium-high heat, then reduce the heat to low and simmer soup, covered, for 1½–1¾ hours, or until beans are tender. Season to taste with salt and pepper, and serve immediately. Season adult portions with hot red pepper sauce and additional mustard, if desired.

Note: The soup can be prepared up to 2 days in advance and refrigerated, tightly covered. Reheat it over low heat, covered, until hot, stirring occasionally.

Variation:
- Substitute bacon fat for the vegetable oil, substitute Chicken Stock (recipe on page 55) for the Vegetable Stock, and add ½ pound diced baked ham or cut up hot dogs to the soup after it has cooked for 1 hour.

The reason why this soup takes a long time to cook even though the beans have soaked is that acid ingredients, such as the tomatoes and vinegar in this recipe, retard beans from softening.

Low-Country Fish Soup

"Low-country" is the nickname given the area of coast from Savannah, Georgia, to Charleston, South Carolina. This mildly flavored soup is similar to a bisque, and it's a good way to encourage kids to eat more fish.

Yield: 4–6 servings | **Active time:** 20 minutes | **Start to finish:** 40 minutes

- 2 hard-cooked eggs, peeled
- 3 tablespoons unsalted butter
- 3 scallions, white parts and 3 inches of green tops, rinsed, trimmed, and chopped
- 1 celery rib, rinsed, trimmed, and chopped
- 3 tablespoons all-purpose flour
- 2 teaspoons paprika
- 2 cups Seafood Stock (recipe on page 58) or purchased stock
- ¼ cup dry sherry
- 2 tablespoons tomato paste
- 3 cups half-and-half or whole milk
- 1 (10-ounce) package frozen mixed vegetables, thawed
- 1¼ pounds thick white-fleshed fish fillets, rinsed and cut into 1-inch cubes
- Salt and freshly ground black pepper to taste

Adult additions:
- 2–3 tablespoons additional tablespoons dry sherry
- Hot red pepper sauce to taste

1. Separate whites and yolks of eggs. Chop whites, and set aside. Push yolks through a fine sieve, and set aside.
2. Heat butter in a 4-quart saucepan over medium heat. Add scallions and celery, and cook, stirring frequently, for 3 minutes, or until scallions are translucent.
3. Reduce the heat to low, stir in flour, and cook for 2 minutes, stirring constantly. Add paprika, and cook for 30 seconds. Whisk in stock, sherry, and tomato paste. Stir well to dissolve tomato paste.
4. Bring to a boil over high heat, then reduce the heat to medium, and cook soup, uncovered, for 10 minutes.

5. Add milk, mixed vegetables, and fish. Bring back to a boil, and simmer soup, covered, for 5 minutes, or until fish is cooked through and flakes easily. Season to taste with salt and pepper, and serve immediately. Add additional sherry and hot pepper sauce to adult portions, if desired.

Note: The soup can be prepared up to 2 days in advance and refrigerated, tightly covered. Reheat it over low heat, covered, until hot, stirring occasionally.

Variation:
- Substitute 1 pint fresh minced clams for the fish, and substitute 1 (8-ounce) bottle clam juice for the Seafood Stock.

> If your kids think that something tastes "too fishy," try substituting Chicken Stock (recipe on page 55) or Vegetable Stock (recipe on page 57) for the Seafood Stock. That switch will create a dish with a much less distinct fish flavor.

New England Clam Chowder

Early chowder recipes call for everything from beer to ketchup, but not milk. What we know as New England chowder dates from the mid-nineteenth century. My version includes celery and herbs, which create a more complex flavor.

Yield: 4–6 servings | **Active time:** 20 minutes | **Start to finish:** 40 minutes

> 1 pint fresh minced clams
> 4 tablespoons (½ stick) unsalted butter, divided
> 2 medium onions, peeled and diced
> 2 celery ribs, rinsed, trimmed, and diced
> 1 (8-ounce) bottle clam juice
> 2 medium redskin potatoes, scrubbed and cut into ¾-inch dice
> 2 tablespoons chopped fresh parsley
> 1 bay leaf
> 1 teaspoon dried thyme
> Salt and freshly ground black pepper to taste
> 3 tablespoons all-purpose flour
> 3 cups whole milk

1. Drain clams in a sieve over a bowl, reserving the juice in the bowl. Press down with the back of a spoon to extract as much liquid as possible from clams.
2. Melt 2 tablespoons butter in a 2-quart saucepan over medium heat. Add onions and celery, and cook, stirring frequently, for 3 minutes, or until onions are translucent. Add bottled clam juice and reserved clam juice to the pan, along with potatoes, parsley, bay leaf, thyme, salt, and pepper. Bring to a boil, reduce the heat to low, and simmer, covered, for 10–12 minutes, or until potatoes are tender.
3. While mixture simmers, melt remaining butter in a small saucepan over low heat. Stir in flour and cook, stirring constantly, for 2 minutes. Raise the heat to medium and whisk in milk. Bring to a boil, whisking frequently, and simmer for 2 minutes.
4. Stir thickened milk into the pot with vegetables, and add clams. Bring to a boil, reduce the heat to low, and simmer, uncovered, for 3 minutes. Remove and discard bay leaf, season to taste with salt and pepper, and serve immediately.

Note: The soup can be made up to 2 days in advance and refrigerated, tightly covered. Reheat it over low heat, covered, until hot, stirring occasionally.

Variations:
- Start by cooking ¼ pound bacon until crisp, and then use 2 tablespoons bacon fat instead of butter to sauté the vegetables. Crumble the bacon and add along with the clams.
- Add 1 cup cooked corn kernels along with the clams.
- Cook ½ green bell pepper, finely chopped, along with the onions.

Eating clam chowder can become a great history lesson for your kids about the Pilgrims and the founding of New England, or even later history. This might be a good time to introduce them to Herman Melville's *Moby Dick* if they're old enough.

Old-Fashioned Chicken Noodle Soup

Wait until your kids taste this favorite when it doesn't come out of a can! It will be a whole new world for them. Tender egg noodles and a variety of vegetables in a richly flavored homemade stock are the hallmarks of this American classic.

Yield: 4–6 servings | **Active time:** 15 minutes | **Start to finish:** 35 minutes

8 cups Chicken Stock (recipe on page 55) or purchased stock
1 cup medium egg noodles
2 tablespoons unsalted butter
1 medium onion, peeled and diced
2 celery ribs, rinsed, trimmed, and sliced
2 carrots, peeled and sliced
3 tablespoons chopped fresh parsley
1 teaspoon dried thyme
1 bay leaf
2–3 cups diced cooked chicken
$2/3$ cup frozen cut green beans, thawed
$1/2$ cup frozen peas, thawed
Salt and freshly ground black pepper to taste

1. Place stock in a saucepan over high heat. Bring to a boil, and cook for 10 minutes, or until stock is reduced by $1/4$. If using purchased stock, you will probably not have to add additional salt at the end of the cooking process.

2. Bring a large pot of salted water to a boil over high heat. Add egg noodles and cook according to package directions until al dente. Drain, and set aside.

3. While water heats, melt butter in a 4-quart saucepan over medium-high heat. Add onion, celery, and carrots, and cook, stirring frequently, for 3 minutes, or until onion is translucent. Add stock, parsley, thyme, and bay leaf, and bring to a boil over high heat.

4. Reduce the heat to low and simmer soup, uncovered, for 15 minutes, or until vegetables are tender. Add chicken, green beans, and peas, and simmer for 5 minutes. Remove and discard bay leaf, stir in noodles, and season to taste with salt and pepper. Serve immediately.

Note: The soup can be prepared up to 2 days in advance and refrigerated, tightly covered. Reheat it over low heat, covered, until hot, stirring occasionally. Refrigerate noodles separately, and add them when reheating soup.

Variations:
- Add 1 (14.5-ounce) can diced tomatoes, undrained, to the soup.
- Add 1 (15-ounce) can garbanzo beans, kidney beans, or cannellini beans, drained and rinsed.
- Substitute cooked pasta or rice for the egg noodles.
- Substitute 2 large redskin potatoes, scrubbed and cut into ³/₄-inch dice, for the noodles. Add the potatoes to the soup along with the stock.

You can save money on your energy bills if every time you bring a pot of salted water to a boil to cook pasta or noodles you cover the pot until it begins to boil. Five minutes here and there add up on your gas or electric bill.

Indian Red Lentil Soup (Mulligatawny)

This soup is a wonderful way to introduce kids to the flavor of curry because it's a mild undertone in this vivid red soup. While the soup originated in India, it became very popular in England during the nineteenth century.

Yield: 4–6 servings | **Active time:** 20 minutes | **Start to finish:** 55 minutes

3 tablespoons unsalted butter
1 large onion, peeled and chopped
2 carrots, peeled and chopped
2 celery ribs, rinsed, trimmed, and chopped
2 garlic cloves, peeled and minced
1 tablespoon grated fresh ginger
1 tablespoon curry powder
6 cups Chicken Stock (recipe on page 55) or purchased stock
1 tablespoon tomato paste
²/₃ cup red lentils, rinsed
2 tablespoons chopped fresh parsley
1 bay leaf
2–3 cups diced cooked chicken
¹/₃ cup heavy cream
Salt and cayenne to taste

1. Heat butter in a 4-quart saucepan over medium-high heat. Add onion, carrots, celery, garlic, and ginger. Cook, stirring frequently, for 3 minutes, or until onion is translucent. Add curry powder, and cook for 1 minute, stirring constantly.

2. Add stock and tomato paste, and stir well to dissolve tomato paste. Add lentils, parsley, and bay leaf, and bring to a boil over high heat, stirring occasionally. Reduce the heat to low, and simmer soup, covered, for 30 minutes, or until lentils are very tender.

3. Remove and discard bay leaf. Puree soup in a food processor fitted with the steel blade or in a blender.

4. Return soup to the pan, and add chicken and cream. Heat for 3 minutes to warm chicken, then season to taste with salt and cayenne, and serve immediately.

Note: The soup can be prepared up to 2 days in advance and refrigerated, tightly covered. Reheat it over low heat, covered, until hot, stirring occasionally.

Variation:
- For a change, you can give this soup Middle Eastern flavor. Substitute 1 tablespoon ground coriander and 2 teaspoons ground cumin for the ginger and curry powder.

Many recipes call for just 1–2 tablespoons of tomato paste, which is why we all find moldy cans hidden on the back of a refrigerator shelf from time to time. That's a silly waste of money, and the tomato paste in tubes is much more expensive. The answer is to measure out 1-tablespoon portions, and freeze them on a sheet of plastic wrap. Once frozen, transfer them to a heavy resealable plastic bag.

Chili Soup with Beans

Just tell your kids that this soup is like chili con carne or taco filling if that will help as a sales tool. It has all the same seasonings, plus nutritious beans. Serve it with some warm corn or whole wheat tortillas and a tossed salad.

Yield: 4–6 servings | **Active time:** 20 minutes | **Start to finish:** 1 hour

SOUP

3 tablespoons olive oil, divided
³/₄ pound ground chuck
1 large onion, peeled and diced
1 large green bell pepper, seeds and ribs removed, and diced
1 celery rib, rinsed, trimmed, and diced
2 garlic cloves, peeled and minced
1 tablespoon smoked Spanish paprika
1 tablespoon chili powder
1 teaspoon ground cumin
¹/₂ teaspoon dried oregano
4 cups Beef Stock (recipe on page 56) or purchased stock
1 (14.5-ounce) can diced tomatoes, undrained
1 (4-ounce) can diced mild green chiles, drained
2 tablespoons tomato paste
2 (15-ounce) cans red kidney beans, drained and rinsed
Salt and freshly ground black pepper to taste

Adult additions:

1–2 chipotle chiles in adobo sauce, finely chopped
2–3 tablespoons chopped fresh cilantro

GARNISH

1 cup crushed corn tortilla chips
¹/₂–³/₄ cup grated cheddar cheese
¹/₂–³/₄ cup sour cream or plain yogurt

1. Heat 1 tablespoon oil in a 4-quart saucepan over medium-high heat. Add beef, breaking up lumps with a fork, and cook for 2–3 minutes, or until beef browns and no pink remains. Remove beef from the pan with a slotted spoon, and set aside. Discard fat from the pan.

2. Heat remaining oil over medium-high heat. Add onion, green bell pepper, celery, and garlic. Cook, stirring frequently, for 3 minutes, or until onion is translucent. Add paprika, chili powder, cumin, and oregano, and cook for 1 minute, stirring constantly.

3. Return beef to the pan and add stock, tomatoes, chiles, and tomato paste. Stir well to dissolve tomato paste, and bring to a boil over medium-high heat.

4. Reduce the heat to low, and simmer soup, covered, for 20 minutes. Add beans, and cook for an additional 20 minutes. Season to taste with salt and pepper, and serve immediately. Season adult portions with chipotle chiles and cilantro, if desired. Pass bowls of tortilla chips, cheddar cheese, and sour cream or yogurt separately.

Note: The soup can be prepared up to 2 days in advance and refrigerated, tightly covered. Reheat it over low heat, covered, until hot, stirring occasionally.

Variation:

- Substitute ground turkey for the ground beef, and substitute Chicken Stock (recipe on page 55) for the Beef Stock.

Beefy Vegetable Soup

Here's another sure-fire hit with kids. There's a cornucopia of vegetables in this soup and they're all recognizable. It's a hearty soup that's very mildly seasoned.

Yield: 4–6 servings | **Active time:** 15 minutes | **Start to finish:** 1 hour

1 pound boneless chuck roast, trimmed and cut into ³/₄-inch cubes

3 tablespoons vegetable oil, divided

1 medium onion, peeled and diced

1 garlic clove, peeled and minced

4 cups Beef Stock (recipe on page 56) or purchased stock

1 (14.5-ounce) can diced tomatoes, undrained

½ pound redskin potatoes, scrubbed and cut into ³/₄-inch dice

1 large carrot, peeled and diced

1 parsnip, peeled and diced

2 celery ribs, rinsed, trimmed, and diced

2 tablespoons chopped fresh parsley

1 teaspoon dried thyme

1 bay leaf

³/₄ cup fresh corn kernels or frozen corn kernels, thawed

³/₄ cup frozen cut green beans, thawed

Salt and freshly ground black pepper to taste

Adult additions:

3 tablespoons chopped fresh parsley

3 garlic cloves, peeled and minced

1 teaspoon grated lemon zest

1. Rinse beef and pat dry with paper towels. Heat ½ of oil in a 4-quart saucepan over medium-high heat. Brown beef on all sides, remove beef from the pan with a slotted spoon, and set aside. Discard fat from the pan.

2. Heat remaining oil in the pan over medium-high heat. Add onion and garlic, and cook, stirring frequently, for 3 minutes, or until onion is translucent.

3. Return beef to the pan, and add stock, tomatoes, potatoes, carrot, parsnip, celery, parsley, thyme, and bay leaf. Bring to a boil over medium-high heat, then reduce the heat to low and simmer soup, covered, for 30–40 minutes, or until beef is tender.

4. Add corn and green beans, and simmer for 5 minutes. Remove and discard bay leaf, season to taste with salt and pepper, and serve immediately. For adult portions, combine parsley, garlic, and lemon zest in a small bowl, and sprinkle over soup, if desired.

Note: The soup can be prepared up to 2 days in advance and refrigerated, tightly covered. Reheat it over low heat, covered, until hot, stirring occasionally.

Variation:
- Substitute boneless, skinless chicken thighs, cut into ¾-inch cubes, for the beef and Chicken Stock (recipe on page 55) for the Beef Stock.

> The easiest way to dice celery is to cut it into thin lengthwise strips first. Then stack the strips on your cutting board horizontally, and dice them into small pieces.

Potato Soup with Ham and Vegetables

Ham is a wonderful meat to cook when it's on sale because it can add both flavor and protein to myriad soups and other dishes; it's also a favorite with kids. This soup is enriched by some cream at the end of the cooking time.

Yield: 4–6 servings | **Active time:** 20 minutes | **Start to finish:** 45 minutes

> 3 tablespoons unsalted butter
> 1 medium onion, peeled and chopped
> 6 scallions, white parts and 3 inches of green tops, rinsed, trimmed, and sliced
> 1 carrot, peeled and diced
> 1 celery rib, rinsed, trimmed, and diced
> 4 cups Chicken Stock (recipe on page 55) or purchased stock
> 3 large baking potatoes, peeled and cut into ¾-inch dice
> 2 tablespoons chopped fresh parsley
> ½ teaspoon dried thyme
> 1 bay leaf
> ½ pound baked ham, trimmed and cut into ½-inch dice
> ½ cup frozen peas, thawed
> 1 cup half-and-half or whole milk
> Salt and freshly ground black pepper to taste

1. Heat butter in a 4-quart saucepan over medium-high heat. Add onion, scallions, carrot, and celery. Cook, stirring frequently, for 3 minutes, or until onion is translucent.
2. Add stock, potatoes, parsley, thyme, and bay leaf. Bring to a boil over high heat, then reduce the heat to low, and simmer soup, covered, for 20 minutes, or until vegetables are tender. Add ham, peas, and half-and-half or milk, and simmer for an additional 5 minutes.
3. Remove and discard bay leaf, and season to taste with salt and pepper. Serve immediately.

Note: The soup can be prepared up to 2 days in advance and refrigerated, tightly covered. Reheat it over low heat, covered, until hot, stirring occasionally.

Variation:
- Substitute smoked turkey or cooked chicken for the ham.

Chicken Stock

Richly flavored, homemade chicken stock is as important as good olive oil in my kitchen. Once you've gotten into the habit of "keeping stocked," you'll appreciate the difference that it makes in all soups and sauces. And making it is as easy as boiling water.

Yield: 4 quarts | **Active time:** 10 minutes | **Start to finish:** 4 hours

    6 quarts water
    5 pounds chicken bones, skin, and trimmings
    4 celery ribs, rinsed and cut into thick slices
    2 onions, trimmed and quartered
    2 carrots, trimmed, scrubbed, and cut into thick slices
    2 tablespoons whole black peppercorns
    6 garlic cloves, peeled
    4 sprigs parsley
    1 teaspoon dried thyme
    2 bay leaves

1. Place water and chicken pieces in a large stockpot, and bring to a boil over high heat. Reduce the heat to low, and skim off foam that rises during the first 10–15 minutes of simmering. Simmer stock, uncovered, for 1 hour, then add celery, onions, carrots, peppercorns, garlic, parsley, thyme, and bay leaves. Simmer for 2½ hours.
2. Strain stock through a fine-meshed sieve, pushing with the back of a spoon to extract as much liquid as possible. Discard solids, spoon stock into smaller containers, and refrigerate. Remove and discard fat from surface of stock, then transfer stock to a variety of container sizes.

Note: The stock can be refrigerated and used within 3 days, or it can be frozen for up to 6 months.

Variation:
- Substitute the same amount of turkey giblets and necks as chicken pieces.

Beef Stock

While beef stock is not specified as often as chicken stock in recipes, it is the backbone to certain soups and the gravy for stews and roasts. If you bone your own roasts to make beef stew, you'll have a cache of trimmings and bones to make it, too.

Yield: 2 quarts | **Active time:** 15 minutes | **Start to finish:** 3½ hours

- 2 pounds beef trimmings (bones and fat) or inexpensive beef shank
- 3 quarts water
- 1 carrot, trimmed, scrubbed, and cut into thick slices
- 1 medium onion, peeled and sliced
- 1 celery rib, trimmed and sliced
- 1 tablespoon whole black peppercorns
- 3 sprigs fresh parsley
- 1 teaspoon dried thyme
- 2 garlic cloves, peeled
- 2 bay leaves

1. Preheat the oven broiler, and line a broiler pan with heavy-duty aluminum foil. Broil beef for 3 minutes per side, or until browned. Transfer beef to a large stockpot, and add water. Bring to a boil over high heat. Reduce the heat to low, and skim off foam that rises during the first 10–15 minutes of simmering. Simmer for 1 hour, uncovered, then add carrot, onion, celery, peppercorns, parsley, thyme, garlic, and bay leaves. Simmer for 3 hours.

2. Strain stock through a fine-meshed sieve, pushing with the back of a spoon to extract as much liquid as possible. Discard solids, and spoon stock into smaller containers. Refrigerate; remove and discard fat from surface of stock.

Note: The stock can be refrigerated and used within 3 days, or it can be frozen for up to 6 months.

Variation:
- Substitute 1 large ham bone for the beef trimmings.

Vegetable Stock

You may think it's not necessary to use vegetable stock if making a vegetarian dish that includes the same vegetables, but that's not the case. Using stock creates a much more richly flavored dish that can't be replicated by increasing the quantity of vegetables cooked in it.

Yield: 2 quarts | **Active time:** 10 minutes | **Start to finish:** 1 hour

- 2 quarts water
- 2 carrots, scrubbed, trimmed, and thinly sliced
- 2 celery ribs, trimmed and sliced
- 1 small onion, peeled and thinly sliced
- 1 tablespoon whole black peppercorns
- 3 sprigs fresh parsley
- 1 teaspoon dried thyme
- 2 garlic cloves, peeled
- 1 bay leaf

1. Pour water into a stockpot, and add carrots, celery, onion, peppercorns, parsley, thyme, garlic, and bay leaf. Bring to a boil over high heat, then reduce the heat to low and simmer stock, uncovered, for 1 hour.
2. Strain stock through a fine-meshed sieve, pushing with the back of a spoon to extract as much liquid as possible. Discard solids, and allow stock to cool to room temperature. Spoon stock into smaller containers, and refrigerate.

Note: The stock can be refrigerated and used within 3 days, or it can be frozen for up to 6 months.

Seafood Stock

Seafood stock is a great reason to make friends with the head of the fish department of your supermarket, or with a fishmonger, if you're lucky enough to live near a store devoted to fish and seafood. You can arrange in advance to have them save you bodies if the store cooks lobster meat, or purchase them at minimal cost. The same is true with fish bones, if a store actually fillets the fish on site.

Yield: 2 quarts | **Active time:** 15 minutes | **Start to finish:** 1³/₄ hours

> 3 lobster bodies (whole lobsters from which the tail and claw meat has been removed) or shells from 3 pounds raw shrimp
> 3 quarts water
> 1 cup dry white wine
> 1 carrot, scrubbed, trimmed, and cut into 1-inch chunks
> 1 medium onion, peeled and sliced
> 1 celery rib, rinsed, trimmed, and sliced
> 1 tablespoon whole black peppercorns
> 3 sprigs fresh parsley
> 1 teaspoon dried thyme
> 2 garlic cloves, peeled
> 1 bay leaf

1. If using lobster bodies, pull top shell off 1 lobster body. Scrape off and discard feathery gills, then break body into small pieces. Place pieces into a stockpot, and repeat with remaining lobster bodies. If using shrimp shells or fish bones, rinse and place in the stockpot.

2. Add water, wine, carrot, onion, celery, peppercorns, parsley, thyme, garlic, and bay leaf. Bring to a boil over high heat, then reduce the heat to low and simmer stock, uncovered, for 1¹/₂ hours.

3. Strain stock through a fine-meshed sieve, pushing with the back of a spoon to extract as much liquid as possible. Discard solids, and allow stock to cool to room temperature. Spoon stock into smaller containers, and refrigerate.

Note: The stock can be refrigerated and used within 3 days, or it can be frozen for up to 6 months.

Variation:

- Substitute 2 pounds bones and skin from firm-fleshed white fish such as halibut, cod, or sole, for the lobster bodies or shrimp shells.

Seafood stock is perhaps the hardest to make if you don't live near the coast. A good substitute is bottled clam juice. Use it in place of the water, and simmer it with vegetables and wine to intensify its flavor.

Chapter 4:
$1 Snack Attacks

Your food budget includes everything you eat, not just what you eat for dinner. And that includes snacks. These can be after-school snacks for the kids or something adults munch with a glass of wine before dinner. They all cost money, and many times it's in the snack category that expensive convenience products slip into your grocery cart.

In the same way that people on a diet have to guard against "mindless munching," people trying to reduce their food budgets need to be on the alert for snack foods with empty nutrition. But there are lots of alternatives that are both lower in cost and higher in nutrition, and those are the recipes you'll find in this chapter.

There's a big bunch of smoothies, as well as some easy-to-make homemade granola bars to increase the amount of whole grains in your kids' diets in a way they'll love. While a smoothie at a drive-through can be a few dollars for a small portion, that's what a whole batch will cost when made at home—and you'll be using fresh rather than processed ingredients. The chapter ends with some fast dips to keep around with a bowl of carrot sticks or some baked tortilla chips.

SMOOTH SAILING

Smoothies have been around since the first blender was invented in the 1930s, and owners experimented by whirring up fruit with some ice. As early as the 1950s, West Coast health food stores were selling thick pureed fruit drinks.

The term *smoothie* was first used in a blender cookbook in the early 1960s, but the drink genre left California beaches and gained nationwide popularity during the past decade. Smoothies are a great afternoon snack for kids, and a good liquid breakfast as well. It's a lot easier to sip a smoothie than it is to maneuver a bowl of cereal while driving!

Thick texture is one hallmark of a smoothie. Most of the time that comes from pureed fruit. The higher the water content, the less texture a fruit adds to the drink. For example, a banana will make a smoothie far thicker than cubes of watermelon. Watermelon is more than 90 percent water, so once it's pureed, you have a lot of pink water without much texture.

There are various categories of ingredients that go into a smoothie:

- There has to be something liquid in the blender to make a smoothie, which is something you drink from a glass and don't eat with a spoon from a bowl. The larger the percentage of liquid to solid, the thinner the smoothie will be.

- The more frozen ingredients, the thicker the smoothie will become. If you like really chilled and really thick smoothies, then use more frozen ingredients. If you like the drinks only slightly thicker than a glass of juice, then use all your ingredients right from the refrigerator.

- While some fruits, such as bananas, give smoothies a creamy texture, this role is usually played by the binder. Sometimes called a liaison (not to be confused with an illicit meeting), a binder can be a dairy product, such as yogurt, frozen yogurt, or ice cream. It can also be non-dairy, such as silken tofu or frozen tofu.

You'll notice that all the smoothie recipes in this chapter blend the liquid and soft ingredients first, and then incorporate the frozen ones. There's a reason for this. Even the most powerful blender will take a long time to crush frozen ingredients. It has a much easier time if there's a liquid matrix to keep the frozen ingredients moving inside the blender jar.

If you're using ingredients in a different form than those listed in the recipe, reverse the order or use. For example, if the banana you're using is frozen rather than at room temperature, add it at the end of the recipe rather than at the beginning. Just remember that the rule is that frozen ingredients go last.

When making modifications in a smoothie recipe, make sure that the substitutions are within the same category of ingredient. For example, it's fine to substitute frozen yogurt for ice cream, but not to substitute frozen yogurt for the fruit.

BLENDER BASICS

All you need to make a smoothie is a blender, and most kitchens have one of those. If you're really a devotee of smoothies, you might consider a variation on the blender called a smoothie maker. The blender beaker has a spigot in the bottom for serving the viscous beverage.

While a blender looks innocuous, it's definitely a machine that you need to approach with caution. Here are some tips on using it safely:

- Always keep a hand on the top of the lid to ensure that it won't fly off.

- Never put your hands in the blender jar, and make sure the blades have stopped moving before inserting a spatula into the jar.

- Use only rubber spatulas, not metal spoons or knives.

- Turn off the blender completely before removing the lid, and allow the liquid to stop moving.

- Cut food into small, uniform-size pieces. An ice cube is about the largest size that should be added to the blender.

- Never fill a blender more than two-thirds full. The motor in the blender moves the liquid around, and pushes it above the level of the liquid when the motor is not running, so never make it too full.

Chocolate Banana Smoothie

Bananas are consistently the most affordable fruit, regardless of where you live, and along with their low price, they are also universally in stock. A great hit with kids is to flavor the creamy banana with chocolate.

Yield: 4–6 servings | **Active time:** 10 minutes | **Start to finish:** 10 minutes

- 1½ cups whole milk
- ½ cup chocolate syrup
- 3 tablespoons unsweetened cocoa powder
- 2 cups sliced banana
- 1 cup chocolate frozen yogurt
- ½ cup chocolate shavings (optional)

1. Combine milk, chocolate syrup, cocoa powder, and banana in a blender or smoothie maker. Blend on high speed for 45 seconds, or until mixture is pureed and smooth.
2. Add frozen yogurt, and blend on high speed again until mixture is smooth. Serve immediately, garnished with chocolate shavings, if using.

Note: Smoothies can be made up to 2 hours in advance, and refrigerated in the blender beaker. Blend the mixture briefly again before serving.

Variation:
- Substitute caramel syrup and vanilla frozen yogurt, and omit the cocoa powder.

Rather than always having to use a measuring cup for ice cream or frozen yogurt, measure the capacity of your ice cream scoop. From that point on you will know the volume and will not have to dirty another cup.

Cinnamon Banana Smoothie

The subtle flavor of cinnamon is one of the first spices that kids identify and like. This smoothie has the flavor of banana bread, with the addition of healthful honey rather than refined sugar as the sweetener.

Yield: 4–6 servings | **Active time:** 10 minutes | **Start to finish:** 10 minutes

    1 (8-ounce) container vanilla yogurt or 1 cup vanilla frozen yogurt
    ½ cup heavy cream
    ⅓ cup honey
    1 tablespoon lemon juice
    ½ teaspoon ground cinnamon
    2 large bananas, sliced and frozen

1. Combine yogurt, cream, honey, lemon juice, and cinnamon in a blender or smoothie maker. Blend on high speed for 45 seconds, or until mixture is pureed and smooth.
2. Add banana, and blend on high speed again until banana is pureed and mixture is smooth. Serve immediately.

Note: Smoothies can be made up to 2 hours in advance, and refrigerated in the blender beaker. Blend the mixture briefly again before serving.

Variation:

• Substitute ½ cup pure maple syrup for the honey.

A banana with an almost black skin is a banana with great flavor and sweetness, but if you have too many on the counter, do not despair. Puree the fruit and freeze it in ice cube trays. You are then set not only for smoothies, but also to make banana bread or muffins on a moment's notice.

Banana Colada Smoothie

There is a theory that foods that grow on the same soil taste good when eaten together, and tropical pineapple and coconut provide validation of this point. In addition to being complementary flavors, these two fruits are both high in fiber.

Yield: 4–6 servings | **Active time:** 10 minutes | **Start to finish:** 10 minutes

> 1 cup light coconut milk
> 1 cup diced pineapple, chilled
> 1/3 cup lightly packed shredded coconut
> 1/2 teaspoon pure rum extract
> 2 cups frozen banana slices

1. Combine coconut milk, pineapple, coconut, and rum extract in a blender or smoothie maker. Blend on high speed for 45 seconds, or until mixture is pureed and smooth.
2. Add banana slices, and blend on high speed again until mixture is smooth. Serve immediately.

Note: Smoothies can be made up to 2 hours in advance, and refrigerated in the blender beaker. Blend the mixture briefly again before serving.

Variation:

• Substitute coconut extract for the rum extract, and substitute whole milk for the light coconut milk.

Tropical Pineapple Banana Smoothie

Silken tofu is the form of this nutrition-rich soy product best suited to make non-dairy smoothies. In this case, there's a bit of crystallized ginger adding sparkle to the flavor of the drink.

Yield: 4–6 servings | **Active time:** 10 minutes | **Start to finish:** 10 minutes

> 1 cup pineapple juice, chilled
> 1/2 cup silken tofu
> 2 tablespoons crystallized ginger
> 1 cup diced pineapple
> 1 1/2 cups frozen banana slices

1. Combine pineapple juice, tofu, ginger, and pineapple in a blender or smoothie maker. Blend on high speed for 45 seconds, or until mixture is pureed and smooth.
2. Add banana, and blend on high speed again until mixture is smooth. Serve immediately.

Note: Smoothies can be made up to 2 hours in advance, and refrigerated in the blender beaker. Blend the mixture briefly again before serving.

Variation:
- Substitute mango or papaya for the pineapple, and mango or papaya nectar for the pineapple juice.

Choosing ripe pineapples and ripe melons is always a challenge because nudging the flesh is not a conclusive test, and flesh that is too soft can mean the fruit is spoiled. I have found that the best test is to smell the fruit at the stem end. If it smells sweet, there is a good chance it is ripe.

Banana and Peanut Butter Smoothie

Peanut butter and bananas are a kid-friendly combination if there ever was one. This treat is sweetened with honey, which contains a strong antioxidant, too. Honey is also a natural healing agent, which is why opera singers use it for sore throats.

Yield: 4–6 servings | **Active time:** 10 minutes | **Start to finish:** 10 minutes

    1 cup soy milk
    ½ cup silken tofu
    ¼ cup honey
    ½ cup peanut butter
    ¼ cup sunflower seeds
    ½ teaspoon ground cinnamon
    ½ teaspoon pure vanilla extract
    2 cups frozen banana slices
    Sprinkling of cinnamon for garnish (optional)

1. Combine soy milk, tofu, honey, peanut butter, sunflower seeds, cinnamon, and vanilla in a blender or smoothie maker. Blend on high speed for 45 seconds, or until mixture is pureed and smooth.
2. Add banana, and blend on high speed again until mixture is smooth. Serve immediately, garnished with a sprinkling of cinnamon, if using.

Note: Smoothies can be made up to 2 hours in advance, and refrigerated in the blender beaker. Blend the mixture briefly again before serving.

Variation:
- Substitute dry-roasted peanuts for the sunflower seeds.

If your honey has crystallized and is almost impossible to spoon out, place the jar in a pan of very hot tap water for about 10 minutes and it should become liquid again. Do not place it in the microwave, which can heat it too much.

Spiced Apple Smoothie

This flavorful snack is like drinking an apple pie. It's flavored with a bit of spice, and it includes vanilla frozen yogurt, which is like having that on top of the pie.

Yield: 4-6 servings | **Active time:** 10 minutes | **Start to finish:** 10 minutes

> 1/2 cup apple juice, chilled
> 1/2 cup applesauce, chilled
> 1 large apple, peeled, cored, and diced
> 1/2 teaspoon apple pie spice (or 1/4 teaspoon ground cinnamon and
>   1/4 teaspoon ground nutmeg)
> 1 cup vanilla frozen yogurt or vanilla ice cream
> 1/4 cup granola cereal (optional)

1. Combine apple juice, applesauce, apple, and apple pie spice in a blender or smoothie maker. Blend on high speed for 45 seconds, or until mixture is pureed and smooth.
2. Add frozen yogurt or ice cream, and blend on high speed again until smooth. If using granola, add it and pulse blender on and off at low speed to incorporate, but do not puree granola. Serve immediately.

Note: Smoothies can be made up to 2 hours in advance, and refrigerated in the blender beaker. Blend the mixture briefly again before serving.

Variations:
- Substitute raisins for the granola.
- Add 1/4 cup walnuts to the smoothie mixture.

I like to substitute Chinese five-spice powder for apple pie spice in all my cooking and baking because it has a more complex flavor. Try it some time.

Creamy Strawberry Smoothie

One great aspect of smoothies is that they're a way to get kids to have dairy products other than a glass of milk. This smoothie includes both sour cream and cream cheese; it tastes reminiscent of a cheesecake topped with strawberries.

Yield: 4–6 servings | **Active time:** 10 minutes | **Start to finish:** 10 minutes

    1 (8-ounce) container strawberry yogurt
    1/3 cup sour cream
    1 (3-ounce) package cream cheese
    1/4 cup fruit-only strawberry preserves
    2 1/2 cups sliced strawberries
    3 ice cubes

1. Combine yogurt, sour cream, cream cheese, and strawberry preserves in a blender or smoothie maker. Blend on high speed for 45 seconds, or until mixture is pureed and smooth.
2. Add strawberries and ice cubes, and blend on high speed again until strawberries are pureed and mixture is smooth. Serve immediately.

Note: Smoothies can be made up to 2 hours in advance, and refrigerated in the blender beaker. Blend the mixture briefly again before serving.

Variation:
- You can use almost any yogurt and fruit combination for this recipe, such as peach, raspberry, blueberry, or cherry.

> If you don't have a flavored yogurt, you can always substitute plain yogurt, and then add 2 tablespoons of a fruit jam to the recipe.

PB&J Smoothie

Contrary to their name, peanuts are actually members of the legume family; they are botanically related to lentils and beans and are high in protein. If your kids like a PB&J sandwich, they'll also love this smoothie version.

Yield: 4–6 servings | **Active time:** 10 minutes | **Start to finish:** 10 minutes

    1 (8-ounce) container strawberry yogurt
    1 cup whole milk
    1 cup shelled peanuts
    ¼ cup fruit-only strawberry jam
    1½ cups frozen strawberries
    4 strawberry fans for garnish (optional)

1. Combine yogurt, milk, peanuts, and strawberry jam in a blender or smoothie maker. Blend on high speed for 45 seconds, or until mixture is pureed and smooth.
2. Add strawberries, and blend on high speed again until mixture is smooth. Serve immediately, garnished with strawberry fans, if using.

Note: Smoothies can be made up to 2 hours in advance, and refrigerated in the blender beaker. Blend the mixture briefly again before serving.

Variation:
* Substitute blueberry yogurt, blueberry jam, and blueberries for the strawberry foods in this smoothie.

Here's how to select the best peanuts in their shells. If possible, pick up a peanut and shake it, looking for two signs of quality. First, it should feel heavy for its size. Second, it should not rattle, since a rattling sound suggests that the peanut kernels have dried out. Additionally, the shells should be free from cracks, dark spots, and insect damage.

No-Bake Peanutty Granola Bars

This snack is a healthy version of the one made with marshmallows and Rice Krispies. It contains whole grains in addition to the cereal, and the peanut butter and honey—both loaded with nutrients—keep it together.

Yield: 16 bars | **Active time:** 15 minutes | **Start to finish:** 30 minutes

½ cup honey
½ cup peanut butter (smooth or chunky)
3 tablespoons vegetable oil
2 tablespoons firmly packed dark brown sugar
½ teaspoon ground cinnamon
½ teaspoon pure vanilla extract
Pinch of salt
2 cups quick oats (not instant or old-fashioned)
2 cups rice cereal, such as Rice Krispies
¾ cup chopped dried apricots
½ cup chopped peanuts
Vegetable oil spray

1. Line a 9 x 13-inch baking dish with heavy-duty aluminum foil, and grease the foil with vegetable oil spray.
2. Combine honey, peanut butter, oil, brown sugar, cinnamon, vanilla, and salt in a small saucepan. Cook over medium heat, stirring occasionally, for 3–5 minutes, or until mixture begins to simmer.
3. While mixture cooks, combine oats, rice cereal, dried apricots, and peanuts in a mixing bowl. Pour peanut butter mixture over dry ingredients, and stir well to coat evenly. Scrape mixture into the prepared pan, and pack it in evenly with a rubber spatula.
4. Refrigerate for 15–20 minutes, or until mixture is set. Cut into 16 pieces with a sharp serrated knife.

Note: The bars can be made up to 4 days in advance and stored in an airtight tin at room temperature.

Variations:

• Substitute chopped dried dates or raisins for the dried apricots.

Cranberry Granola Bars

What masquerade as granola bars in supermarkets are cookies with a bit of crunch; just look at the label and you'll see that the first ingredient is usually all-purpose white flour. On the other hand, these inexpensive and delicious bars are full of nutritious whole grains.

Yield: 16 bars | **Active time:** 15 minutes | **Start to finish:** 55 minutes

> ½ cup chopped walnuts
> 6 tablespoons (¾ stick) unsalted butter, sliced
> ¼ cup firmly packed dark brown sugar
> ¼ cup honey
> ¼ teaspoon ground ginger
> Pinch of salt
> 2 cups old-fashioned oats
> ½ cup dried cranberries
> ½ cup toasted wheat germ
> Vegetable oil spray

1. Preheat the oven to 350°F. Line a 9-inch-square baking pan with heavy-duty aluminum foil, and grease the foil with vegetable oil spray. Toast walnuts on a baking sheet for 5–7 minutes, or until lightly browned. Remove nuts from the oven, and transfer them to a mixing bowl.

2. While nuts bake, combine butter, brown sugar, honey, ginger, and salt in a small saucepan. Place the pan over medium heat, and cook, stirring frequently, until mixture comes to a boil. Remove the pan from the heat.

3. Add oats, cranberries, and wheat germ to the mixing bowl with nuts. Pour butter mixture over dry ingredients, and stir well to coat evenly.

4. Scrape mixture into the prepared pan, and pack it in evenly with a rubber spatula. Bake for 30 minutes, or until top is golden brown. Cool for 10 minutes on a wire rack, then remove from the pan. Cut into 16 pieces with a sharp serrated knife while still warm.

Note: The bars can be made up to 4 days in advance and stored in an airtight tin at room temperature.

Variation:

- Substitute pecans or peanuts for the walnuts, and substitute raisins or chopped dried apricots for the dried cranberries.

It's important to cut granola bars while they're still warm. They don't contain the usual leavening agents as do bar cookies, so they're very dense. That makes them difficult to cut once they've cooled completely.

Super-Crunchy Raisin Granola Bars

All the dry ingredients in these baked treats are toasted first, which makes them extra crunchy, and brings out their best flavor.

Yield: 16 bars | **Active time:** 15 minutes | **Start to finish:** 1 hour

1½ cups old-fashioned oats
1 cup slivered blanched almonds
½ cup raw sunflower seeds
½ cup wheat germ
6 tablespoons (¾ stick) unsalted butter, sliced
½ cup honey
¼ cup pure maple syrup
1 teaspoon pure vanilla extract
Pinch of salt
¾ cup raisins
Vegetable oil spray

1. Preheat the oven to 350°F. Line a 9-inch-square baking pan with heavy-duty aluminum foil, and grease the foil with vegetable oil spray.
2. Combine oats, almonds, sunflower seeds, and wheat germ on a baking sheet. Bake mixture, stirring occasionally, for 12–15 minutes, or until ingredients are browned. Transfer mixture to a mixing bowl, and reduce the oven temperature to 300°F.
3. While mixture bakes, combine butter, honey, maple syrup, vanilla, and salt in a small saucepan. Place the pan over medium heat, and cook, stirring frequently, until mixture comes to a boil. Remove the pan from the heat.
4. Pour butter mixture over dry ingredients, add raisins, and stir well to coat evenly.
5. Scrape mixture into the prepared pan, and pack it in evenly with a rubber spatula. Bake for 25 minutes, or until top is golden brown. Cool for 10 minutes on a wire rack, then remove from the pan. Cut into 16 pieces with a sharp serrated knife while still warm.

Note: The bars can be made up to 4 days in advance and stored in an airtight tin at room temperature.

Variation:
- Substitute pecans or walnuts for the almonds.

Mexican Kidney Bean Dip

In addition to using it as a delicious dip, you can mound this aromatic blend of beans and spices onto corn chips, top it with some grated cheese, and broil it briefly into nachos.

Yield: 1½ cups | **Active time:** 15 minutes | **Start to finish:** 15 minutes

¼ cup olive oil

1 small onion, peeled and chopped

2 garlic cloves, peeled and minced

1 (15-ounce) can kidney beans, drained and rinsed

¼ cup sour cream

3 tablespoons lime juice

1 teaspoon ground coriander

1 teaspoon ground cumin

½ teaspoon dried oregano

Salt and freshly ground black pepper to taste

Adult addition:

1 small jalapeño or serrano chile, seeds and ribs removed, and finely chopped

1. Heat olive oil in a large skillet over medium-high heat. Add onion and garlic, and cook, stirring frequently, for 3 minutes, or until onion is translucent. Scrape mixture into a mixing bowl, and set aside.
2. Combine beans, sour cream, lime juice, coriander, cumin, and oregano in a food processor fitted with a steel blade, and puree until smooth. Scrape mixture into the mixing bowl with vegetables, season to taste with salt and pepper, and stir well. Add chile to adult portion, if desired. Serve immediately.

Note: The dip can be prepared up to 2 days in advance and refrigerated, tightly covered. Allow it to reach room temperature before serving.

Variation:

• Substitute plain nonfat yogurt for the sour cream.

Hot Tex-Mex Sweet Potato Dip

The inherent sweetness of the bright orange potatoes is balanced by some characteristic Southwestern seasoning in this healthful dip.

Yield: 4–6 servings | **Active time:** 15 minutes | **Start to finish:** 1¾ hours

3 large sweet potatoes

2 scallions, white parts and 3 inches of green tops, rinsed, trimmed, and chopped

2 tablespoons chopped fresh cilantro

1 ripe plum tomato, cored, seeded, and chopped

1 garlic clove, peeled and minced

2 tablespoons balsamic vinegar

2 tablespoons olive oil

Salt and freshly ground black pepper to taste

¼–½ cup water

Adult addition:

1 jalapeño or serrano chile, seeds and ribs removed, and finely chopped

1. Preheat the oven to 400°F, and line a baking sheet with aluminum foil. Prick sweet potatoes with a fork and bake for 1–1½ hours, or until very soft. Cool potatoes slightly and scoop flesh into a large microwave-safe mixing bowl.

2. Add scallions, cilantro, tomato, garlic, balsamic vinegar, and olive oil to the potatoes. Mash well with a potato masher, and season to taste with salt and pepper. If too thick, add water until mixture reaches desired consistency. Add chile to adult portions, if desired.

3. Cover the dip with plastic wrap and microwave on medium (50 percent power) for 2–3 minutes, or until dip is hot, stirring well after each minute.

Note: The sweet potatoes can be baked up to 2 days in advance and refrigerated, tightly covered. Also, the dip can be made up to 1 day in advance, and refrigerated, tightly covered. Reheat it in a microwave oven until hot.

Variation:

- Substitute 1 (15-ounce) can solid-pack pumpkin for the sweet potatoes.

What we call sweet potatoes are not really potatoes, although they are a tuberous vegetable. A related tuber is the yam. Often confused with sweet potatoes, yams have lighter colored flesh that is actually sweeter than that of sweet potatoes. They are native to Africa and are not readily available. They are more often found in Asian and Hispanic markets.

Asian Carrot Dip

Kids love carrots, plain and simple. And these sweet vegetables, loaded with healthful beta-carotene, become the basis for this dip that's fast to make, too.

Yield: 4–6 servings | **Active time:** 10 minutes | **Start to finish:** 10 minutes

>   5 carrots, peeled and sliced
>   1/3 cup mayonnaise
>   3 tablespoons hoisin sauce*
>   2 tablespoons grated fresh ginger
>   2 tablespoons soy sauce
>   1 tablespoon Asian sesame oil*
>   2 scallions, white parts and 4 inches of green top, rinsed, trimmed, and chopped
>   Freshly ground black pepper to taste

Adult addition:
>   2 garlic cloves, peeled and minced
>   1 small jalapeño or serrano chile, seeds and ribs removed, and finely chopped

1. Combine carrots, mayonnaise, hoisin sauce, ginger, soy sauce, and sesame oil in a food processor fitted with the steel blade or in a blender. Puree until smooth.
2. Stir in scallions, and season to taste with pepper. Serve immediately. For adult portions, add garlic and chile, if desired.

Note: The dip can be prepared up to 2 days in advance and refrigerated, tightly covered. Allow it to reach room temperature before serving.

*Available in the Asian aisle of most supermarkets and in specialty markets.

Chapter 5:
Yankee Doodle and Noodles, Too

One of the definitions of "comfort food" is food with which we're comfortable; it's familiar food. And for us, those dishes are traditional American foods. That's what you'll find in this chapter, and because these foods are universally popular with kids, this is a lengthy chapter.

All regional American food developed as a combination of which ethnic groups joined the Native American population living on the lands, which dishes they brought with them, and what crops the land would support. In New England, the plain foods of the Pilgrims were sweetened with maple syrup, and the French and Spanish settlers to Louisiana adapted their *paella* and *bouillabaisse* to jambalaya and gumbo.

While there are dishes in this chapter for almost all American regions, the Southwestern ones are in Chapter 6, along with authentic Hispanic fare. I felt that the two genres really belonged together.

One difference between the recipes in this chapter and many traditional recipes is that I've significantly cut back on the amount of fat used and added many more vegetables. While the prototypes for some of these foods date back to the eighteenth century, you'll be happy to feed them to twenty-first-century kids.

MEATLOAF IN THE FAST LANE
Just as small pieces of food for a stir-fry cook in less time than a large roast, a meatloaf mixture baked in muffin cups is ready in far less time than in a loaf pan. While the meatloaf recipes in this chapter are written to be baked as one unit, you can change that to speed them up. Another advantage of baking meatloaves as "muffins" is that you can take them to the office for lunch; the muffins don't fall apart the way slices tend to do.

Here's how to do it: Preheat the oven to 400°F, and spray 8–12 muffin cups with vegetable oil spray. Divide the meatloaf mixture into the prepared muffin cups, and bake for 20–25 minutes, or until an instant-read thermometer inserted into the center registers 165°F.

An alternative, if you don't have a muffin pan, is to form the meat mixture into individual "logs" that are about 3 inches high. Bake them at 375°F for 25–30 minutes.

Chesapeake Fish Cakes

While crab cakes are an extravagant treat, by the time the spices and vegetables are added to the mix you can hardly taste the delicate crab, so why not use fish and make them affordable? These are baked rather than fried, so they are a lean dish, too.

Yield: 4–6 servings | **Active time:** 15 minutes | **Start to finish:** 40 minutes

> 1 pound thin white-fleshed fish fillets
> 1 tablespoon Old Bay seasoning
> 1 large egg
> 3 tablespoons mayonnaise
> 3 tablespoons breadcrumbs or cracker meal
> 2 green bell peppers, seeds and ribs removed, and very finely chopped
> 4 scallions, white parts and 3 inches of green tops, rinsed, trimmed, and very finely chopped
> 3 tablespoons chopped fresh parsley
> Vegetable oil spray

1. Preheat the oven to 400°F, cover a baking sheet with heavy-duty aluminum foil, and spray the foil with vegetable oil spray. Rinse fish and pat dry with paper towels. Rub fish with Old Bay, and bake for 10 minutes, or until opaque and flakes easily. Remove fish from the oven, flake it, and set aside to cool. Change the foil on the baking sheet, and spray the new sheet of foil with vegetable oil spray.
2. While fish bakes, combine egg, mayonnaise, and breadcrumbs in a mixing bowl, and whisk until well blended. Stir in green bell peppers, scallions, and parsley. Gently fold in cooked fish.
3. Divide mixture into 8–12 portions. Form mixture into balls and then flatten them on the baking sheet into patties 1-inch thick. Spray tops with vegetable oil spray. Bake for 15–18 minutes, or until lightly brown on top. Serve immediately.

Note: The fish mixture can be prepared 1 day in advance and refrigerated, tightly covered with plastic wrap. Do not form or bake the cakes until just before serving.

Variations:
- Substitute 3 (5-ounce) cans light tuna, drained, for the fresh fish, and add Old Bay seasoning to the mayonnaise mixture.
- Substitute ¾ pound chopped cooked chicken for the fish, and add Old Bay seasoning to the mayonnaise mixture.

Seasoning mixtures such as Old Bay or Cajun seasoning contain both salt and pepper, so don't add additional seasoning when using them in recipes.

Fish Pot Pie

Pot pies are the quintessentially American way to enjoy food; the protein is cooked with assorted vegetables in an herbed cream sauce and then nestled beneath a crispy crust. This one made with fish is just delicious, and very easy to make.

Yield: 4–6 servings | **Active time:** 25 minutes | **Start to finish:** 1¼ hours

> 4 tablespoons (½ stick) unsalted butter, divided
> 1 medium onion, peeled and diced
> 2 carrots, peeled and thinly sliced
> 2 redskin potatoes, scrubbed and cut into ½-inch dice
> 1 cup dry white wine
> 1 cup Seafood Stock (recipe on page 58) or purchased stock
> 1 bay leaf
> 3 tablespoons all-purpose flour
> 1 cup half-and-half
> 2 tablespoons chopped fresh parsley
> 1 teaspoon dried thyme
> Salt and freshly ground black pepper to taste
> 1 pound thick white-fleshed fish fillet, cut into 1-inch cubes
> 1 cup frozen peas, thawed
> 1 Basic Piecrust (recipe on page 244) for a single crust pie, or purchased piecrust sheet
> 1 large egg, lightly beaten

1. Preheat the oven to 400°F.
2. Melt 2 tablespoons butter in a large skillet over medium-high heat. Add onion and cook, stirring frequently, for 3 minutes, or until onion is translucent. Add carrots, potatoes, wine, stock, and bay leaf to the pan. Bring to a boil, then reduce the heat to low and cook vegetables, uncovered, for 10 minutes, or until potatoes are almost tender. Remove and discard bay leaf. Strain and reserve cooking liquid.
3. Melt remaining 2 tablespoons butter in a small saucepan, and stir in flour. Cook over low heat, stirring constantly, for 2 minutes. Whisk in reserved cooking liquid, half-and-half, parsley, and thyme. Bring to a boil, whisking constantly, and simmer sauce for 2 minutes. Season to taste with salt and pepper.

4. Combine sauce, vegetable mixture, fish, and peas in round 2-quart casserole. Cover the pan with aluminum foil, and bake for 20 minutes. Remove the casserole from the oven, and fit sheet of piecrust over the top, crimping the edges and trimming off any excess dough. Brush crust with beaten egg, and cut 6 (1-inch) slits to allow steam to escape. Bake pie, uncovered, for 30 minutes, or until crust is brown. Serve immediately.

Note: The vegetable mixture and sauce can be prepared up to 1 day in advance and refrigerated, tightly covered. Do not add seafood to the vegetable and sauce mixture until just before baking, and add 15 minutes to initial baking time if chilled.

Variations:
- Substitute 1 pound cooked chicken or turkey for the fish, and substitute Chicken Stock (recipe on page 55) for the Seafood Stock.
- Substitute 3 (5-ounce) cans tuna, drained and broken into chunks, for the fish.

Crimping, sometimes referred to as fluting, means pinching or pressing two pastry edges together, thereby sealing the dough while forming a decorative edge with fingers, fork, or some other utensil. The pastry for a single-crust pie is crimped by turning it under to form a ridge, then shaping the raised edge into a fancy pattern.

Tuna and Broccoli Mac' and Cheese

All members of my Parents Panel listed broccoli, along with carrots, as a favorite veggie for their kids. In this dish, mildly flavored tuna is also added to what is essentially mac' and cheese.

Yield: 4–6 servings | **Active time:** 20 minutes | **Start to finish:** 50 minutes

½ pound macaroni
3 tablespoons unsalted butter
3 tablespoons all-purpose flour
2 cups half-and-half or whole milk
3 tablespoons chopped fresh parsley
1½ cups grated Swiss cheese, divided
Pinch nutmeg
Salt and freshly ground black pepper to taste
1 (10-ounce) package frozen chopped broccoli, thawed and
   drained
3 (5-ounce) cans light tuna, drained

1. Preheat the oven to 375°F, and grease a 9 x 13-inch baking pan. Bring a large pot of salted water to a boil. Add macaroni, and cook for 2 minutes less than package directions. Drain, and place macaroni in the prepared pan.
2. Melt butter in a saucepan over low heat. Stir in flour, and cook, stirring constantly, for 2 minutes. Whisk in half-and-half or milk and parsley, and bring to a boil over medium-high heat, whisking constantly. Reduce the heat to low, and simmer for 2 minutes. Stir in 1 cup cheese, stirring until cheese melts. Then stir in nutmeg, and season to taste with salt and pepper.
3. Stir broccoli, tuna, and sauce into macaroni, and sprinkle with remaining ½ cup cheese. Bake for 25–30 minutes, or until bubbly. Allow to sit for 5 minutes, then serve immediately.

Note: The dish can be prepared up to baking 2 days in advance and refrigerated, tightly covered. Reheat it, covered with foil, for 15 minutes before removing foil and baking for 25 minutes.

Variations:
- Substitute 2–3 cups cooked diced chicken for the tuna.
- Substitute chopped spinach or cauliflower for the broccoli.
- Substitute cheddar cheese for the Swiss cheese.

Because the tuna is totally cooked, it's possible to prepare this dish in its entirety in advance, but that is not the case when mixing raw protein into cooked food. Raw and cooked food should not be refrigerated together, with the exception of raw eggs; those can be refrigerated with cooked food for up to 24 hours.

Updated Tuna Noodle Casserole

The basic concept of this homey classic is great; what had marred it was its execution with chemical-laden canned soup! But it's fast and easy to make your own cream sauce, and the fresh mushrooms are a great addition.

Yield: 4–6 servings | **Active time:** 15 minutes | **Start to finish:** 45 minutes

> 6 ounces medium egg noodles
> 5 tablespoons unsalted butter, divided
> 1 medium onion, peeled and diced
> 2 celery ribs, rinsed, trimmed, and diced
> ½ pound mushrooms, wiped with a damp paper towel, stemmed, and diced
> ¼ cup all-purpose flour
> 2 cups whole milk
> Salt and freshly ground black pepper to taste
> 3 (5-ounce) cans light tuna, drained and broken into chunks
> 1 (5-ounce) bag potato chips, crushed

1. Preheat the oven to 375°F, and grease a 9 x 13-inch baking pan. Bring a large pot of salted water to a boil, and cook noodles according to package directions. Drain, and return noodles to the pot.
2. Melt 2 tablespoons butter in a large skillet over medium-high heat. Add onion, celery, and mushrooms. Cook, stirring frequently, for 5–7 minutes, or until celery softens. Remove the pan from the heat, and set aside. Add vegetables to the pot with noodles.
3. Melt remaining butter in a saucepan over low heat. Stir in flour, and cook, stirring constantly, for 2 minutes. Slowly whisk in the milk, and bring to a boil over medium heat, whisking constantly. Simmer 1 minute, and season to taste with salt and pepper. Pour sauce into the pot with noodles, and gently fold in tuna.
4. Scrape mixture into the prepared pan, level top with rubber spatula, and sprinkle with potato chips. Cover pan with aluminum foil, and bake for 10 minutes. Remove foil, and bake an additional 20 minutes, or until hot and bubbly. Serve immediately.

Note: The dish can be prepared for baking up to 2 days in advance and refrigerated, tightly covered. Add 10 minutes to covered baking time if the dish is chilled, and do not sprinkle with potato chip crumbs until just before baking.

Variations:
- Add ½ green or red bell pepper, seeds and ribs removed and chopped, to skillet with other vegetables.
- Substitute canned salmon, bones and skin discarded, for the tuna.
- Substitute ¾ pound diced cooked chicken or turkey for the tuna.
- Substitute a flavored potato chip for the plain chips.
- Substitute crushed corn tortilla chips for the potato chips.

Basic Oven-Fried Chicken

Using this easy method, chicken emerges from the oven with skin as crisp as if it was deep-fried on top of the stove, but there's no mess! And you can play with your kids while it bakes, or prepare the rest of dinner.

Yield: 4–6 servings | **Active time:** 10 minutes | **Start to finish:** 35 minutes

> 1 (3½–4-pound) frying chicken, cut into serving pieces with each breast cut in half crosswise
> 1 cup buttermilk
> 2 large eggs, lightly beaten
> 1½ cups finely crushed corn flakes
> ½ cup breadcrumbs
> 1 cup vegetable oil, divided
> 3 tablespoons Cajun seasoning
> Salt and freshly ground black pepper to taste

1. Preheat the oven to 450°F, and place a 10 x 14-inch baking pan in the oven as it heats. Rinse chicken and pat dry with paper towels.
2. Combine buttermilk and eggs in a shallow bowl, and whisk well. Combine crushed corn flakes, breadcrumbs, 2 tablespoons oil, Cajun seasoning, salt, and pepper in a second large bowl, and mix well.
3. Dip chicken pieces into buttermilk mixture, letting any excess drip back into the bowl. Dip pieces into breadcrumb mixture, coating all sides. Refrigerate chicken for a minimum of 10 minutes.
4. Add remaining oil to hot baking dish, and heat in the oven for 3 minutes. Add chicken pieces and turn gently with tongs to coat all sides with oil. Bake for a total of 25 minutes, turning pieces gently with tongs after 15 minutes, or until chicken registers 165°F on an instant-read thermometer and is cooked through and no longer pink. Remove chicken from the pan, and pat with paper towels. Serve immediately.

Note: The chicken can be prepared for baking up to 6 hours in advance and refrigerated, tightly covered.

Variations:

- Use seasoned Italian breadcrumbs, and add ¼ cup freshly grated Parmesan cheese to the mixture.
- Use rice cereal in place of the corn flakes.
- Use fluffy panko breadcrumbs, and season them with herbes de Provence.
- Substitute smoked Spanish paprika for the Cajun seasoning, and season egg mixture to taste with salt and pepper.

It's best to refrigerate foods prior to frying to allow time for the crumbs to adhere. This brief time bonds the egg and breading so the crumbs are less likely to fall off when the food is fried. This is also true if food is coated with flour before its egg dip.

Baked Apple Chicken

This is a new version of barbecued chicken that can be done in the oven, and kids love it because it has the flavor of apple juice—one of their favorite drinks. Serve it with coleslaw and potato salad.

Yield: 4–6 servings | **Active time:** 15 minutes | **Start to finish:** 1 hour

> 1 (3½–4-pound) frying chicken, cut into serving pieces with each breast cut in half crosswise
> Salt and freshly ground black pepper to taste
> 1 (6-ounce) can apple juice concentrate, thawed
> ½ cup bottled chili sauce
> ½ cup cider vinegar
> 2 tablespoons vegetable oil
> 2 teaspoons dried sage

Adult additions:
> Hot red pepper sauce to taste
> 2 garlic cloves, peeled and minced

1. Preheat the oven to 400°F, and line a baking sheet with heavy-duty aluminum foil. Rinse chicken, pat dry with paper towels, and sprinkle with salt and pepper. Arrange chicken skin side down on the baking sheet.

2. Combine apple juice concentrate, chili sauce, vinegar, oil, and sage in a small bowl, and stir well. Add hot red pepper sauce and garlic to adult portion of glaze, if desired. Brush chicken with glaze.

3. Bake chicken for 15 minutes, brushing it once more with glaze. Turn chicken pieces skin side up with tongs. Brush tops of chicken pieces with glaze. Return chicken to the oven, and bake for an additional 30 minutes, brushing it every 10 minutes with glaze, or until chicken registers 165°F on an instant-read thermometer and is cooked through and no longer pink. Serve immediately.

Note: The dish can be prepared up to 2 days in advance and refrigerated, tightly covered. Reheat it, covered, in a 350°F oven for 20–25 minutes, or until hot. It can also be served cold.

Variation:

- Substitute orange juice concentrate or lemonade concentrate for the apple juice concentrate.

Chili sauce is not related to chili powder. This chunky condiment is a blending of tomatoes, sweet chiles, onions, green peppers, vinegar, sugar, and spices. While the texture will be smooth, ketchup is the best replacement.

Potato-Crusted Chicken

This is my favorite way to eat a boneless chicken breast. Since it's marinated with herbs and garlic and then sandwiched between two potato pancakes, it could be called a "chicken latke." Serve it with a tossed salad.

Yield: 4–6 servings | **Active time:** 25 minutes | **Start to finish:** 40 minutes

> 1 pound boneless, skinless chicken breast halves
> Salt and freshly ground black pepper to taste
> 1 teaspoon dried thyme
> 2 tablespoons olive oil
> 2 garlic cloves, peeled and minced
> 1 large onion, peeled and diced
> 2 large eggs
> 1 cup all-purpose flour, divided
> 1½ pounds russet potatoes, peeled
> 2–3 cups vegetable oil for frying

1. Rinse chicken and pat dry with paper towels. Pound chicken between 2 sheets of plastic wrap to an even thickness of ½ inch. Cut chicken into 4–6 serving pieces. Mix salt, pepper, thyme, olive oil, and garlic together in a small bowl. Spread this mixture on the chicken.

2. Puree onion, eggs, ½ cup flour, salt, and pepper in a food processor fitted with the steel blade or in a blender. Scrape mixture into a mixing bowl. Shred the potatoes in a food processor fitted with a coarse shredding disk or through the large holes of a box grater. Squeeze out excess moisture, and mix potatoes into onion mixture. Push a sheet of plastic wrap directly onto the surface of the mixture to prevent discoloration.

3. To cook, heat 1 inch of oil in a large skillet over high heat to a temperature of 375°F. Dust chicken with remaining flour, shaking off any excess over the sink or a garbage can, and coat on both sides with ⅓ inch of the potato mixture. Fry for 5–6 minutes per side, turning pieces gently with a slotted spatula, or until golden. Drain on paper towels, and serve immediately.

Note: The potato mixture and chicken can be prepared up to 6 hours in advance and refrigerated, tightly covered. Do not fry it until just prior to serving.

Variation:
- Substitute sweet potatoes for the russet potatoes.

Potatoes have a lot of liquid, although we think of them as a dry vegetable. That's why it's important when making any sort of potato pancake or french fry that the moisture is pressed out of them.

Biscuit-Topped Chicken Pie

Biscuits are to the American South what a baguette is to France; it wouldn't be a day without them. In this case, they're flavored with cheddar cheese, and used to top a pot pie made with lots of vegetables in a creamy sauce.

Yield: 4–6 servings | **Active time:** 20 minutes | **Start to finish:** 50 minutes

CHICKEN

- 4 tablespoons ($\frac{1}{2}$ stick) unsalted butter, divided
- 1 small onion, peeled and chopped
- 1 cup Chicken Stock (recipe on page 55) or purchased stock
- 1 large carrot, peeled and thinly sliced
- 2 celery ribs, rinsed, trimmed, and thinly sliced
- 1 large russet potato, peeled and cut into $\frac{3}{4}$-inch dice
- 2 tablespoons chopped fresh parsley
- 1 teaspoon dried thyme
- 1 bay leaf
- 1 cup frozen peas, thawed
- 3 tablespoons all-purpose flour
- 1 cup half-and-half
- Salt and freshly ground black pepper to taste
- 2–3 cups diced cooked chicken

BISCUITS

- $1\frac{1}{2}$ cups all-purpose flour
- 2 teaspoons baking powder
- $\frac{1}{2}$ teaspoon baking soda
- Salt to taste
- 2 tablespoons cold unsalted butter, cut into bits
- 1 cup grated sharp cheddar cheese
- 1 cup sour cream

1. Preheat oven to 400°F, and grease a 9 x 13-inch baking pan.
2. Heat 2 tablespoons butter in a medium skillet over medium-high heat. Add onion, and cook, stirring frequently, for 3 minutes, or until onion is translucent. Add stock, carrot, celery, potato, parsley, thyme,

and bay leaf to the skillet. Bring to a boil, reduce heat to low, and simmer, partially covered, for 8–10 minutes, or until potato is tender. Add peas to the skillet, and cook 1 minute. Strain mixture, reserving stock. Remove and discard bay leaf, and transfer vegetables to the prepared baking pan.

3. Heat remaining butter in a saucepan over low heat. Stir in flour, and cook, stirring constantly, for 2 minutes. Whisk in reserved stock, and bring to a boil over medium-high heat, whisking constantly. Add half-and-half, and simmer 2 minutes. Season to taste with salt and pepper. Add chicken to the pan with vegetables, and stir in sauce. Season to taste with salt and pepper.

4. While vegetables simmer, prepare biscuits. Sift flour, baking powder, baking soda, and salt together into a mixing bowl. Cut in butter using a pastry blender, two knives, or your fingertips until mixture resembles coarse meal. Add cheddar and sour cream, and stir until it forms a soft but not sticky dough. Knead dough gently on a lightly floured surface, roll or pat it out 1/2-inch thick, and cut out 8–12 rounds with a floured cookie cutter. Arrange biscuits on top of filling, and bake for 30–40 minutes, or until biscuits are brown and filling is bubbling. Allow to stand for 5 minutes, then serve.

Note: The chicken mixture can be prepared up to 2 days in advance and refrigerated, tightly covered. Reheat mixture in a saucepan or in the microwave oven before topping with biscuits, and do not make biscuit dough until just prior to serving.

Variations:
- Substitute Swiss cheese for the cheddar cheese.
- For a Southwestern pot pie, substitute cilantro for the parsley and substitute 2 tablespoons chili powder for the thyme. Add 1 (4-ounce) can chopped mild green chiles, drained, to the filling, and substitute jalapeño Jack cheese for the cheddar cheese in the biscuits.

Chicken Croquettes

Croquettes of all types have been used as a way to stretch leftovers for centuries; they are basically a thick white sauce into which cooked food is folded, formed into patties, and fried. I adore them, and they are very easy to make.

Yield: 4–6 servings | **Active time:** 20 minutes | **Start to finish:** 1½ hours, including 1 hour to chill mixture

CROQUETTES

4 tablespoons (½ stick) unsalted butter
1 small onion, peeled and finely chopped
1 cup all-purpose flour, divided
⅔ cup whole milk
⅔ cup Chicken Stock (recipe on page 55) or purchased stock
3 cups finely chopped cooked chicken
2 tablespoons chopped fresh parsley
1 tablespoon Cajun seasoning
2 large eggs, lightly beaten
2 tablespoons water
1 cup plain breadcrumbs
3 cups vegetable oil for frying

SAUCE

1 cup Basic White Sauce (recipe on page 33)
¾ cup grated Swiss cheese
Salt and freshly ground black pepper to taste

1. Heat butter in a saucepan over medium heat. Add onion and cook, stirring frequently, for 2 minutes. Add ⅓ cup flour, reduce the heat to low, and cook for 2 minutes, stirring constantly. Whisk in milk and stock, and bring to a boil over medium heat, whisking constantly. Reduce the heat to low, and simmer sauce for 2 minutes. Remove the pan from the heat.

2. Stir chicken, parsley, and Cajun seasoning into sauce, and transfer mixture to a 9 x 13-inch baking pan. Spread mixture evenly, and refrigerate for 30 minutes, or until cold, loosely covered with plastic wrap.

3. Place remaining flour on a sheet of plastic wrap, combine eggs and water in a shallow bowl, and place breadcrumbs on another sheet of plastic wrap. With wet hands, form chilled mixture into 2-inch balls, and flatten balls into patties. Dust patties with flour, dip into egg mixture, and dip into breadcrumbs, pressing to ensure crumbs adhere. Refrigerate patties for 30 minutes.
4. While patties chill, make Basic White Sauce. Add cheese, and stir until cheese melts. Season to taste with salt and pepper, and keep warm.
5. Heat oil in a deep-sided skillet over medium-high heat to 375°F. Add patties, being careful not to crowd the pan. Cook for a total of 3–5 minutes, or until browned. Remove croquettes from the pan with a slotted spoon, and drain well on paper towels. Serve immediately, passing sauce separately.

Note: The croquettes can be prepared for frying up to 1 day in advance and refrigerated, tightly covered. They can also be fried in advance; reheat them in a 375°F oven for 10–12 minutes, or until hot and crusty again.

Variation:
- Make croquettes with turkey and follow this recipe.
- Make croquettes with chopped ham, omitting the Cajun seasoning and adding 1 teaspoon dried sage, salt, and pepper.
- Make them with chopped fish or seafood—salmon, cod, halibut, shrimp, and crab all work well—and omit the Cajun seasoning and add 1 tablespoon Old Bay seasoning.

The best way to test the temperature of oil is with a thermometer; they're sometimes called candy thermometers, but they test all high-temperature liquids. If you don't have one, drop a small cube of bread into the oil. The oil should bubble furiously and the cube should toast within 10 seconds if it has reached 375°F.

New England Turkey Meatloaf

This version of meatloaf, made with lean ground turkey, is topped with cranberry sauce, and flavored with the same herbs I use on a roast turkey. Serve it with mashed potatoes and some succotash.

Yield: 4–6 servings | **Active time:** 15 minutes | **Start to finish:** 1¼ hours

    2 tablespoons vegetable oil
    1 large onion, peeled and chopped
    2 garlic cloves, peeled and minced
    1 celery rib, rinsed, trimmed, and chopped
    1 pound ground turkey
    2 large eggs, lightly beaten
    ½ cup plain breadcrumbs
    2 tablespoons chopped fresh parsley
    1 tablespoon dried sage
    1 teaspoon dried thyme
    Salt and freshly ground black pepper to taste
    ½ cup canned whole berry cranberry sauce
    Vegetable oil spray

1. Preheat the oven to 375°F, line a 9 x 13-inch baking pan with aluminum foil, and grease the foil with vegetable oil spray.
2. Heat oil in a medium skillet over medium-high heat. Add onion, garlic, and celery. Cook, stirring frequently, for 5 minutes, or until onion softens. Scrape mixture into a mixing bowl. Add turkey, eggs, breadcrumbs, parsley, sage, thyme, salt, and pepper. Mix well to combine.
3. Form mixture into a loaf in the prepared pan, and spread the top with cranberry sauce.
4. Bake the meatloaf for 1 hour or until an instant-read thermometer that is inserted into the center of the loaf registers 165°F. Serve immediately.

Note: The meatloaf can be made up to 2 days in advance and refrigerated, tightly covered. Reheat it in a 350°F oven, covered with foil, for 20–30 minutes, or until hot. It's also delicious served cold!

Variations:

- Substitute ground pork for the ground turkey.
- Using the method outlined above, substitute Italian breadcrumbs for the plain, and 2 teaspoons Italian seasoning for the thyme and sage. Add ¼ cup freshly grated Parmesan cheese to the turkey mixture, and top the meatloaf with chunky marinara sauce instead of cranberry sauce.
- To "sneak" more vegetables into your kids, add 1 grated carrot to the turkey mixture.

Even though this meatloaf bakes for a considerable amount of time, it's still important to cook the vegetables until they soften to achieve the right texture for the dish.

Sloppy Joes

While the exact origins of this American classic are not known, recipes for this indeed sloppy dish date back to the early 1940s, and by the 1960s, it was a fixture in every school cafeteria. While served on toasted hamburger buns, this is definitely "fork food."

Yield: 4–6 servings | **Active time:** 15 minutes | **Start to finish:** 30 minutes

> 3 tablespoons olive oil, divided
> 1 pound lean ground beef
> 1 medium onion, peeled and chopped
> 2 garlic cloves, peeled and minced
> 1 large green bell pepper, seeds and ribs removed, and chopped
> 2 tablespoons chili powder
> 1 cup ketchup
> 1 cup Beef Stock (recipe on page 56) or purchased stock
> 2 tablespoons Worcestershire sauce
> Salt and freshly ground black pepper to taste

Adult addition:

> ½–1 teaspoon hot red pepper sauce

TO SERVE

> 4–6 hamburger buns, split and toasted
> 1½–2 cups shredded iceberg lettuce, rinsed and dried

1. Heat 1 tablespoon oil in a saucepan over medium-high heat. Add beef, breaking up lumps with a fork, and cook for 3–5 minutes, or until no pink remains. Remove beef from the pan with a slotted spoon, and set aside. Discard fat from the pan.
2. Heat remaining oil in the pan over medium-high heat. Add onion, garlic, and green bell pepper, and cook, stirring frequently, for 3 minutes, or until onion is translucent. Add chili powder, and cook for 1 minute, stirring constantly.
3. Return beef to the pan, and add ketchup, stock, and Worcestershire sauce. Bring to a boil, reduce the heat to medium, and cook for 10–15 minutes, stirring occasionally, or until slightly thickened. Season to taste with salt and pepper, and add hot red pepper sauce to the adult portions, if desired.

4. To serve, mound beef mixture on bottom half of toasted buns, top with lettuce, and replace tops of buns. Serve immediately.

Note: The beef mixture can be made up to 2 days in advance and refrigerated, tightly covered. Reheat it slowly over low heat, covered, stirring occasionally.

Variation:
- Substitute ground turkey for the ground beef.

Any food that you serve on a bun can be piled into a taco shell or rolled in a tortilla as well—especially if your kids like these other forms better.

Cheeseburger Meatloaf

It's all here in one dish, including the pickles and mayo you would use to top the burger, along with ketchup and—of course—the cheese. Serve it with a tossed salad or coleslaw.

Yield: 4–6 servings | **Active time:** 15 minutes | **Start to finish:** 1¼ hours

> 2 tablespoons vegetable oil
> 1 medium onion, peeled and chopped
> 1 small carrot, peeled and grated
> 1 garlic clove, peeled and minced
> 1 large egg
> ¼ cup mayonnaise
> 3 tablespoons sweet pickle relish
> 1 cup grated sharp cheddar cheese, divided
> ½ cup plain breadcrumbs
> 1 teaspoon dry mustard powder
> Salt and freshly ground black pepper to taste
> 1 pound ground chuck
> ⅓ cup ketchup
> Vegetable oil spray

1. Preheat the oven to 375°F, line a 9 x 13-inch baking pan with aluminum foil, and grease the foil with vegetable oil spray.
2. Heat oil in a medium skillet over medium-high heat. Add onion, carrot, and garlic, and cook, stirring frequently, for 5 minutes, or until onion softens.
3. While onion cooks, combine egg, mayonnaise, and pickle relish in a mixing bowl, and whisk well. Add ½ cup cheese, breadcrumbs, mustard, salt, and pepper, and whisk well again. Add onion mixture and beef, and mix well to combine. Form mixture into a loaf in the prepared pan, and spread the top with ketchup.
4. Bake meatloaf for 40 minutes, then sprinkle top of loaf with remaining cheese. Bake for an additional 20 minutes, or until an instant-read thermometer inserted into the center of the loaf registers 165°F. Serve immediately.

Note: The meatloaf can be made up to 2 days in advance and refrigerated, tightly covered. Reheat it in a 350°F oven, covered with foil, for 20–30 minutes, or until hot. It's also delicious served cold!

Variations:
- Cook 4–6 slices bacon until partially cooked, and lay bacon on top of ketchup.
- Substitute ground turkey for the ground beef.

The easiest way to break apart a whole head of garlic is to slam the root end onto the countertop. It should then separate easily into cloves.

Basic Italian-American Meatballs

I really couldn't decide whether to put this recipe in this chapter or in Chapter 7, Mediterranean Madness, and decided that because it's not authentically Italian it should go here. It may not be authentic, but it's pleased generations of American kids.

Yield: 4–6 servings | **Active time:** 20 minutes | **Start to finish:** 50 minutes

2 tablespoons olive oil
1 small onion, peeled and finely chopped
3 garlic cloves, peeled and minced
$\frac{1}{4}$ teaspoon crushed red pepper flakes
1 large egg
3 tablespoons whole milk
$\frac{2}{3}$ cup seasoned Italian breadcrumbs
$\frac{1}{3}$ cup freshly grated Parmesan cheese
$\frac{1}{3}$ cup grated whole-milk mozzarella cheese
3 tablespoons chopped fresh parsley
1 teaspoon Italian seasoning
$\frac{1}{2}$ teaspoon dried thyme
$\frac{1}{2}$ pound ground pork
$\frac{1}{2}$ pound ground chuck
Salt and freshly ground black pepper to taste
2 cups Herbed Tomato Sauce (recipe on page 32) or purchased marinara sauce
Vegetable oil spray

1. Preheat the oven broiler, line a rimmed baking sheet with heavy-duty aluminum foil, and spray the foil with vegetable oil spray.
2. Heat oil in a large skillet over medium-high heat. Add onion, garlic, and red pepper flakes, and cook, stirring frequently, for 3 minutes, or until onion is translucent.
3. Combine egg and milk in a mixing bowl, and whisk until smooth. Add breadcrumbs, Parmesan cheese, mozzarella cheese, parsley, Italian seasoning, and thyme, and mix well.
4. Add onion mixture, pork, and beef, season to taste with salt and pepper, and mix well again. Make mixture into $1\frac{1}{2}$-inch meatballs, and arrange meatballs on the prepared pan. Spray tops of meatballs with vegetable oil spray.

5. Broil meatballs 6 inches from the broiler element, turning them with tongs to brown all sides. While meatballs brown, heat Herbed Tomato Sauce in the skillet in which the vegetables cooked.

6. Remove meatballs from the baking pan with a slotted spoon, and add meatballs to sauce. Bring to a boil, and simmer meatballs, covered, over low heat, turning occasionally with a slotted spoon, for 15 minutes. Season to taste with salt and pepper, and serve immediately.

Note: The meatball mixture can be prepared up to 1 day in advance and refrigerated, tightly covered. Also, the dish can be cooked up to 2 days in advance and refrigerated, tightly covered. Reheat in a 350°F oven, covered, for 15–20 minutes, or until hot.

Variations:
- For traditional spaghetti and meatballs, just cook ½–1 pound of your favorite pasta, and pass some freshly grated Parmesan cheese on the side.
- Cut the cooked meatballs into small pieces and use them to top a pizza.
- For a meatball sandwich, make an indentation in the center of a roll or section of bread to accommodate the size of the meatballs. Then top the meatballs with grated or sliced mozzarella cheese and bake the sandwich in a 375°F oven for 10–12 minutes, or until meatballs are hot and cheese melts.

You've probably noticed that I use a lot of aluminum foil, and, no, I don't own stock in any company that makes it. Lining any pan destined for the oven with aluminum foil cuts cleanup time significantly. The only times not to use it are when you are working on top of the stove or when you plan to use the drippings in an oven pan to make gravy.

Southern Baked Pork Chops with Cornbread

This is a great all-in-one meal, with a cornbread stuffing that serves as a pillow on which sit tender pork chops and a tomato sauce that blankets it all. Serving coleslaw reinforces the Southern theme for the kids.

Yield: 4–6 servings | **Active time:** 20 minutes | **Start to finish:** 1½ hours

1¼ pounds boneless pork loin, cut into ½-inch-thick slices
2 tablespoons olive oil
3 tablespoons unsalted butter
1 medium onion, peeled and chopped
2 celery ribs, rinsed, trimmed, and chopped
1 small green bell pepper, seeds and ribs removed, and chopped
2 tablespoons chopped fresh parsley
½ teaspoon dried thyme
2 cups crumbled cornbread
1 large egg, lightly beaten
Salt and freshly ground black pepper to taste
1 teaspoon chili powder
1 (14.5-ounce) can diced tomatoes, undrained
1 (8-ounce) can tomato sauce
1 bay leaf

1. Preheat the oven to 350°F, and grease a 9 x 13-inch baking pan. Rinse pork, and pat dry with paper towels.
2. Heat oil in a large skillet over medium-high heat. Brown pork on both sides, and set aside.
3. Discard fat from the skillet, and melt butter over medium heat. Add onion, celery, and green bell pepper, and cook, stirring frequently, for 5–7 minutes, or until vegetables soften. Stir in parsley and thyme, and transfer ½ of vegetables to a mixing bowl.
4. Add cornbread and egg to the mixing bowl, season to taste with salt and pepper, and stir well. Spread stuffing evenly on the bottom of the prepared pan.
5. Add chili powder, tomatoes, tomato sauce, and bay leaf to vegetables remaining in the skillet. Bring to a boil over medium-high heat, then reduce the heat to medium and simmer sauce, uncovered, for 5–7 minutes, or until reduced by ¼. Remove and discard bay leaf, and season to taste with salt and pepper.

6. Arrange pork on top of cornbread, and spoon sauce evenly over pork. Cover the pan with aluminum foil, and bake for 1 hour, or until pork is very tender.

Note: The dish can be prepared up to 2 days in advance and refrigerated, tightly covered. Reheat it, covered, in a 350°F oven for 20–25 minutes, or until hot.

Variation:
- Substitute boneless, skinless chicken thighs for the pork chops.

This recipe is a perfect example of how spending a moment of time can save you money. Boneless pork chops, which are boneless pork loin cut into slices, are always more expensive than buying a whole roast, and the slices might not even be the correct width. Whole pork loins are frequently on sale, so cut one up yourself.

Southern Barbecued Pork Sandwiches

This recipe makes true barbecue, the noun and not the verb. The meat is so tender it falls apart, and the sauce is somewhat hot. Once piled on the roll and topped with coleslaw, your meal is done.

Yield: 4-6 servings | **Active time:** 20 minutes | **Start to finish:** 2³/₄ hours

PORK

1¹/₂ pounds boneless country pork ribs, cut into 2-inch sections

3 tablespoons vegetable oil

1 large onion, peeled and chopped

1 green bell pepper, seeds and ribs removed, and chopped

2 garlic cloves, peeled and minced

2 tablespoons smoked Spanish paprika

1 tablespoon chili powder

1 teaspoon dry mustard powder

³/₄ cup ketchup

¹/₂ cup Chicken Stock (recipe on page 55) or purchased stock

¹/₃ cup cider vinegar

¹/₃ cup firmly packed dark brown sugar

3 tablespoons Worcestershire sauce

Salt and freshly ground black pepper to taste

Adult addition:

Hot red pepper sauce to taste

1-2 tablespoons additional cider vinegar

TO SERVE

4-6 rolls of your choice, split and toasted

1-1¹/₂ cups coleslaw (your favorite recipe or purchased)

1. Preheat the oven to 350°F.
2. Rinse pork and pat dry with paper towels. Heat oil in a Dutch oven over medium-high heat. Add pork cubes, and brown well on all sides. Remove pork from the pan with a slotted spoon, and set aside.

3. Add onion, green pepper, and garlic to the Dutch oven, and cook, stirring frequently, for 3 minutes, or until onion is translucent. Stir in paprika, chili powder, and mustard, and cook over low heat for 1 minute, stirring constantly. Add ketchup, stock, vinegar, brown sugar, and Worcestershire sauce, and stir well. Bring to a boil over medium-high heat, stirring frequently.
4. Transfer the pan to the oven. Bake, covered, for $2\frac{1}{2}$ hours, or until pork is falling apart. Tear meat into shreds with 2 forks, and season to taste with salt and pepper. Add hot red pepper sauce and additional vinegar to adult portions, if desired. To serve, mound meat on rolls, and top with coleslaw.

Note: The dish can be prepared up to 2 days in advance and refrigerated, tightly covered. Reheat it over low heat, covered, until hot, stirring occasionally.

Variation:
• Substitute $1\frac{1}{2}$ pounds beef brisket for the pork, and substitute Beef Stock (recipe on page 56) for Chicken Stock. Add 30 minutes to the cooking time.

While the smoked Spanish paprika adds an outdoor nuance to the dish, if you're making it during the summer, sear the ribs on the grill and then braise them for a more pronounced smoked flavor.

Glazed Ham and Pork Meatloaf

I'm a sucker for the sweet and hot glaze served on baked ham, and when you're down to your last few cups of ham, you can replicate the taste with this meatloaf, also made with ground pork to hold it together.

Yield: 4-6 servings | **Active time:** 15 minutes | **Start to finish:** 40 minutes

2 tablespoons unsalted butter
2 tablespoons vegetable oil
1 medium onion, peeled and chopped
½ green bell pepper, seeds and ribs removed, and chopped
1 celery rib, rinsed, trimmed, and chopped
1 garlic clove, peeled and minced
1 large egg, lightly beaten
½ cup plain breadcrumbs
¼ cup milk
¾ cup grated mozzarella cheese
2 tablespoons chopped fresh parsley
1 teaspoon dried thyme
¾ pound ground pork
2 cups finely chopped baked ham
Salt and freshly ground black pepper to taste
¼ cup apricot preserves
3 tablespoons grainy mustard
1 tablespoon grated fresh ginger
Vegetable oil spray

1. Preheat the oven to 400°F, cover a rimmed baking sheet with heavy-duty aluminum foil, and grease the foil with vegetable oil spray.
2. Heat butter and oil in a medium skillet over medium heat. Add onion, green bell pepper, celery, and garlic, and cook, stirring frequently, for 5-7 minutes, or until vegetables soften.
3. While vegetables cook, combine egg, breadcrumbs, milk, mozzarella, parsley, thyme, pork, and ham in a mixing bowl, and mix well. Add vegetables, season to taste with salt and pepper, and mix well again. Form meat mixture into a loaf 5 inches wide and 2 inches high on the prepared baking sheet.

4. Bake meatloaf for 15 minutes. While meatloaf bakes, combine apricot preserves, mustard, and ginger in a small bowl, and stir well. Remove meatloaf from the oven, and spread glaze on top. Bake for an additional 10 minutes, or until an instant-read thermometer registers 165°F when placed in the center. Serve immediately.

Note: The meatloaf can be baked up to 2 days in advance and refrigerated, tightly covered. It can be served cold, or it can be reheated in a 350°F oven, covered with foil, for 20–25 minutes, or until hot.

Variations:
- Substitute ground turkey for the pork, and chopped smoked turkey for the ham.
- Substitute orange marmalade or red currant jelly for the apricot preserves.

Oven-Baked Fish Sticks

Kids love finger foods, and fish sticks—made with real, fresh fish—can fit into that category. These are very crispy because the fish is breaded with fluffy Japanese breadcrumbs. Serve them with coleslaw.

Yield: 4–6 servings | **Active time:** 15 minutes | **Start to finish:** 25 minutes

- 4 tablespoons (½ stick) unsalted butter
- 2 teaspoons lemon juice
- 1½ cups panko breadcrumbs*
- 1¼ pounds thin white-fleshed fish fillets
- Cajun seasoning to taste
- Vegetable oil spray

Adult addition:

- Hot red pepper sauce to taste

1. Preheat the oven to 475°F, line a baking sheet with heavy-duty aluminum foil, and grease the foil with vegetable oil spray.
2. Melt butter in a small saucepan over low heat. Stir in lemon juice, and transfer mixture to a shallow bowl. Place panko in another shallow bowl.
3. Rinse fish and pat dry with paper towels. Cut fish into 1-inch-wide strips. Dip fish into butter, and sprinkle with Cajun seasoning. Then dip both sides of fish into crumbs, pressing fish so that crumbs adhere. Arrange fish on the prepared pan.
3. Bake fish for 10 minutes, or until baked through and flakes easily. Serve immediately. Sprinkle adult portions with hot red pepper sauce, if desired.

Note: The fish can be prepared for baking up to 6 hours in advance and refrigerated, tightly covered.

Variations:
- Substitute Italian breadcrumbs for the panko, and substitute Italian seasoning, salt, and pepper for the Cajun seasoning.
- Substitute crushed corn flakes or crushed toasted rice cereal for the panko.

*Available in the Asian aisle of most supermarkets and in specialty markets.

Chapter 6:
Say ¡Olé!
Hispanic and Southwestern Dishes

Many members of my Parents Panel said that both authentically Hispanic and Americanized dishes lumped under Southwestern cooking were the first ethnic fare beyond spaghetti and meatballs that were a hit with their kids. Those are the recipes you'll find in this chapter.

The amount of spiciness in these dishes can be controlled and customized. Many times I've suggested ways to make them spicier for you, but you can tone them down easily for the kids.

TERRIFIC TACOS

Supermarket taco shells fall into that evil category of convenience food. They are always more expensive than the corn or flour tortillas from which they're made, *and* they're deep-fried. Plus they contain preservatives. So they've got three strikes, and as far as I'm concerned, they're OUT!

It's incredibly easy to make taco shells in the oven using vegetable oil spray. You use very little fat, and you can make them as stiff or soft as your family likes.

There are special gizmos in gourmet stores for oven-baking taco shells. You don't need one, as long as the racks in your oven are clean. And while the gizmo only makes a few at a time, you can make enough for a whole birthday party at once using my method!

Preheat the oven to 375°F. Wrap 6-inch corn tortillas in plastic wrap, and microwave on high (100 percent power) for 30 seconds to 1 minute, depending on the number of tortillas, or until they are hot and pliable. Spray both sides with vegetable oil spray, and then drape the sprayed tortillas over two rungs of your oven rack. Start laying them down from the back to the front.

Bake the shells for 6–8 minutes for a soft shell, and 9–12 minutes for a crisp shell. Various brands of tortillas vary in thickness, so test your shells after the minimum cooking time, and gauge how much longer they should bake.

THOSE PERKY PEPPERS

There are literally hundreds of species of chile pepper, and all owe their ancestry to the Americas. There would be no crushed red pepper in Italian cooking or dried chiles adding fire to Szechwan food except for the exploration of North and South America.

While chiles are found in many cuisines around the world, they are consistently used in Hispanic and Southwestern cooking. I limited the use of fresh chiles to the commonly found jalapeño and serrano species, and the general rule is that the smaller the chile, the hotter the chile. That's why the same number of tiny serrano peppers are used as the much larger jalapeño peppers.

Certain precautions should be exercised in handling fresh chiles because they contain potent oils. Old-fashioned cookbooks call for wearing rubber gloves. That is not necessary. Instead, cut hot chiles on a plate that can be washed in the dishwasher, wash your hands thoroughly with soap and water after handling them, and never touch your skin until you've washed your hands. Do not handle hot chiles under running water, since that spreads the oil vapors upward to your eyes. For the same reason, avoid the steam that rises as you sauté hot chiles.

Two canned products are also frequently used in these recipes:

- Diced or chopped mild green chiles. These are poblano chiles that have been roasted, and they have very little heat. If you don't have any, add some chopped green bell pepper.
- Chipotle chiles in adobo sauce. As you'll see in the recipes in this chapter, these are one of my favorites! They are jalapeño chiles that are dried and then smoked. They add that smoky nuance as well as spice to dishes. The adobo sauce is a less spicy version of hot red pepper sauce, and it has the same smoky notes.

> Most canned beans are very high in sodium, so always taste a mixture made with them before adding salt and pepper. Chances are you'll need very little salt.

Southwestern Pinto Bean Cakes

These hearty vegetarian cakes can be served to the kids on hamburger buns and turned into finger food. They're lightly seasoned, and go well with some sautéed corn or a tossed salad.

Yield: 4–6 servings | **Active time:** 20 minutes | **Start to finish:** 20 minutes

- 6 tablespoons olive oil, divided
- 1 medium onion, peeled and coarsely chopped
- 2 garlic cloves, peeled and minced
- 2 tablespoons chili powder
- 1 tablespoon ground cumin
- 1 teaspoon dried oregano
- 2 (15-ounce) cans pinto beans, drained and rinsed
- 1/4 cup chopped fresh cilantro
- 1/2 cup water
- Salt and freshly ground black pepper to taste

Adult addition:
- 1 chipotle chile in adobo sauce, finely chopped

1. Heat 2 tablespoons olive oil in a heavy, large skillet over medium-high heat. Add onion and garlic, and cook, stirring frequently, for 5 minutes, or until onion softens. Add chili powder, cumin, and oregano and cook, stirring constantly, for 1 minute. Add beans, cilantro, and water. Bring to a boil and simmer mixture, stirring frequently, for 3 minutes.

2. Transfer mixture to a food processor fitted with the steel blade or to a blender and puree. Scrape mixture into a mixing bowl, and season to taste with salt and pepper. Add chipotle chile to adult portions, if desired. Form mixture into 8–12 balls and then flatten balls into patties 1/2-inch thick.

3. Heat remaining 4 tablespoons olive oil in a heavy, large skillet over medium-high heat. Add bean cakes, and cook for 1–2 minutes per side, or until crisp, turning gently with a slotted spatula; this may have to be done in batches. Drain cakes on paper towels.

Note: The bean mixture can be made up to 1 day in advance and refrigerated, tightly covered. The cakes can be fried up to 1 day in advance; reheat them in a 375°F oven for 5–7 minutes, or until hot.

Variation:
- Substitute black beans for the pinto beans.

Vegetable Enchiladas

An enchilada is basically any food rolled in a tortilla that is then baked with a sauce; in this case the filling contains healthful zucchini and corn. The cream sauce is made with both herbs and spices, so it is very flavorful.

Yield: 4–6 servings | **Active time:** 20 minutes | **Start to finish:** 1 hour

4 tablespoons (½ stick) unsalted butter, divided
3 cups coarsely chopped zucchini
1 small onion, peeled and chopped
2 garlic cloves, peeled and minced
1 (10-ounce) package frozen corn, thawed, divided
1 (4-ounce) can diced mild green chiles, drained
¼ cup chopped fresh cilantro
Salt and freshly ground black pepper to taste
2 tablespoons chili powder
2 tablespoons all-purpose flour
2 teaspoons ground cumin
1 teaspoon dried oregano
2½ cups whole milk
1½ cups grated Monterey Jack cheese, divided
8–12 (6-inch) corn tortillas

1. Preheat the oven to 350°F, and grease a 9 x 13-inch baking pan.
2. Melt 2 tablespoons butter in a heavy, large skillet over medium-high heat. Add zucchini, onion, and garlic, and cook, stirring frequently, for 5–7 minutes, or until vegetables soften. Mix in 1 cup corn, chiles, and cilantro, and season to taste with salt and pepper.
3. Melt remaining 2 tablespoons butter in a saucepan over low heat. Whisk in chili powder, flour, cumin, and oregano, and cook 1 minute, stirring constantly. Gradually whisk in milk, and bring to a boil over medium heat, stirring frequently. Reduce the heat to low, and simmer sauce, stirring frequently, for 5 minutes. Add 1 cup cheese, and whisk until smooth. Season to taste with salt and pepper.
4. Spread ¼ cup sauce in the bottom of the prepared pan. Mix ¾ cup sauce into filling. Wrap tortillas in plastic wrap, and microwave on high (100 percent power) for 15–20 seconds, or until warm and pliable.

5. Place generous ⅓ cup filling in center of 1 tortilla, and roll up to enclose filling. Place enchilada in the baking dish, seam side down. Repeat with remaining tortillas and filling. Cover enchiladas with remaining sauce, then sprinkle with remaining ½ cup corn and ½ cup cheese.
6. Cover the pan with foil, and bake 15 minutes. Remove foil and bake an additional 30–35 minutes, or until bubbly. Serve immediately.

Note: The dish can be prepared for baking up to 1 day in advance and refrigerated, tightly covered. Add 10 minutes to the covered baking time if chilled.

Variation:

- Substitute cheddar or jalapeño Jack for some or all of the Monterey Jack cheese.

It's important to wrap tortillas in plastic before softening them in the microwave, because the plastic seals in the inherent moisture. If not covered, the tortillas will instantly turn brittle, and will break when they are rolled.

Baja California Fish Tacos

Fish tacos have been popular in Southern California since their introduction from the Mexican province of Baja California in the 1980s. The creamy dressing is spiked with a hint of smoky chipotle chile.

Yield: 4–6 servings | **Active time:** 15 minutes | **Start to finish:** 15 minutes

FISH

1 pound thin white-fleshed fish fillets
3 tablespoons olive oil
Salt and freshly ground black pepper to taste
1 tablespoon smoked Spanish paprika
Vegetable oil spray

SAUCE

³/₄ cup mayonnaise
¹/₄ cup plain nonfat yogurt
2 tablespoons chopped fresh cilantro
1 tablespoon lime juice
1 chipotle chile in adobo sauce, finely chopped
Adult addition:
1–2 teaspoons adobo sauce

TACOS

8–12 taco shells, made according to the directions given on page
   113 or purchased and heated according to package directions
1¹/₂ cups shredded iceberg lettuce
2–3 ripe plum tomatoes, rinsed, cored, seeded, and chopped

1. Preheat the oven broiler, line a broiler pan with heavy-duty aluminum foil, and grease the foil with vegetable oil spray.
2. Rinse fish and pat dry with paper towels. Cut fish into 1-inch strips, and brush fish with oil. Sprinkle fish on both sides with salt and pepper, and then sprinkle top side with paprika. Broil fish, without turning, for 3–4 minutes, or until cooked through and flakes easily. Remove fish from the broiler.

3. While fish cooks, make sauce. Combine mayonnaise, yogurt, cilantro, lime juice, and chile in a small mixing bowl, and stir well. Add adobo sauce to adult portions, if desired.

4. Place a portion of fish in each taco shell. Toss lettuce with ½ cup sauce, and then place lettuce on top of fish. Garnish each taco with tomato, and serve immediately, passing additional sauce separately.

Note: The sauce can be prepared up to 1 day in advance and refrigerated, tightly covered.

Variation:

- Substitute 3 (5-ounce) cans light tuna, drained and flaked, for the fish, and add the smoked paprika to the sauce.

> Many fish markets sell bits and pieces of fish at a lower cost than whole fillets. For a recipe like this one, feel free to buy them.

Twice-Baked Tex-Mex Tuna Potatoes

Baked potatoes are another food that my Parents Panel said were always popular with kids, and these are lusty; they contain lots of veggies as well as cheese, and the crushed tortilla chips are the final fun factor.

Yield: 4–6 servings | **Active time:** 15 minutes | **Start to finish:** 1¾ hours

4–6 (10-ounce) baking potatoes

½ cup whole milk

2 tablespoons unsalted butter

1½ cups grated taco-flavored cheese blend

2 ripe plum tomatoes, rinsed, cored, seeded, and chopped

2 tablespoons chopped fresh cilantro

3 (5-ounce) cans light tuna, drained and flaked

½ cup crushed corn tortilla chips

Salt and freshly ground black pepper to taste

Adult additions:

1–2 chipotle chiles in adobo sauce, finely chopped

2 scallions, white parts and 3 inches of green tops, rinsed, trimmed, and chopped

1. Preheat the oven to 425°F. Prick each potato with the tines of a heavy meat fork, and arrange potatoes on a baking sheet. Bake for 1–1¼ hours, or until potatoes are tender when pierced with the tip of a paring knife.

2. While potatoes bake, combine milk, butter, and cheese in a small saucepan. Cook over low heat, stirring occasionally, until mixture comes to a simmer and cheese melts. Keep hot.

3. Cut a 1-inch slice off the long side of each potato. Scrape out pulp, leaving a ¼-inch shell, and scrape pulp from top slices. Place pulp in a large bowl. Pour hot cheese mixture over pulp, and mash with a potato masher until smooth.

4. Fold in tomatoes, cilantro, tuna, and crushed tortilla chips. Season to taste with salt and pepper. Add chipotle chile and scallions to adult portions, if desired.

5. Fill potato shells with mixture, and bake for an additional 15–20 minutes, or until hot and top is slightly browned. Serve immediately.

Note: The potatoes can be filled up to 2 days in advance and refrigerated, tightly covered. Bake them, covered with foil, for 15 minutes, then remove the foil, and bake for an additional 15–20 minutes, or until hot.

Variations:
- Substitute 2–3 cups chopped cooked chicken for the tuna.
- Substitute 1 (15-ounce) can kidney beans, drained and rinsed, for the tuna.

Save the potato skins from the slices cut off the tops of the potatoes for snacks. Sprinkle them with some grated cheese and broil them.

Mexican Tuna "Lasagna"

Corn tortillas are used in place of pasta to separate the layers of this dish, which contains creamy ricotta cheese, as well as tuna and healthful beans, in a lively tomato sauce.

Yield: 6–8 servings | **Active time:** 15 minutes | **Start to finish:** 50 minutes

> 3 tablespoons olive oil
> 1 large onion, peeled and diced
> 2 garlic cloves, peeled and minced
> 1 tablespoon chili powder
> 1 teaspoon ground cumin
> 1 teaspoon dried oregano
> 1 (14.5-ounce) can diced tomatoes, drained
> 1 (8-ounce) can tomato sauce
> 1 (15-ounce) can kidney beans, drained and rinsed
> 3 (5-ounce) cans light tuna, drained and flaked
> Salt and freshly ground black pepper to taste
> 1½ cups whole milk ricotta cheese
> 2 large eggs, lightly beaten
> 2 tablespoons canned diced mild green chiles, drained
> 3 tablespoons chopped fresh cilantro
> 12 (6-inch) corn tortillas
> 1½ cups grated Monterey Jack cheese, divided

1. Preheat the oven to 375°F, and grease a 9 x 13-inch baking pan.
2. Heat oil in a large skillet over medium-high heat. Add onion and garlic, and cook, stirring frequently, for 3 minutes, or until onion is translucent. Stir in chili powder, cumin, and oregano. Cook, stirring constantly, for 1 minute. Add tomatoes, tomato sauce, beans, and tuna. Bring to a boil, and simmer 2 minutes. Season to taste with salt and pepper, and set aside.
3. Combine ricotta, eggs, chiles, and cilantro in a mixing bowl. Season to taste with salt and pepper, and stir well.
4. Place ½ of tuna mixture in the bottom of the prepared pan. Top with 6 tortillas, overlapping to cover filling. Spread ricotta cheese mixture on top, and sprinkle with ½ cup Monterey Jack cheese. Layer remaining tortillas, then spread remaining tuna mixture and sprinkle with remaining cheese.

5. Cover the pan with aluminum foil, and bake for 15 minutes. Uncover the pan, and bake for an additional 20 minutes, or until bubbly and cheese melts. Allow to sit for 5 minutes, then serve.

Note: The dish can be prepared up to baking 1 day in advance and refrigerated, tightly covered. Add 10 minutes to the covered bake time if filling is chilled.

Variations:
- Substitute 2–3 cups shredded cooked chicken or turkey for the tuna.
- Substitute 2 medium zucchini, sliced and cooked until tender in 2 tablespoons olive oil, for the tuna.
- Substitute jalapeño Jack for some or all of the Monterey Jack for a spicier dish.

Ricotta cheese is a superb example of recycling. It is made from the whey left over from producing other cheeses, and in Italian its literal meaning is "recooked." It's similar to cottage cheese and farmer cheese in texture.

Chicken Fajitas

Fajitas (pronounced *fah-HEE-taz*) are authentically Mexican, but have also been absorbed into Southwestern cooking. These use chicken, which is then blended with the traditional sautéed onions and peppers.

Yield: 4–6 servings | **Active time:** 25 minutes | **Start to finish:** 25 minutes

CHICKEN

1 pound boneless, skinless chicken breast halves
1/4 cup olive oil, divided
1 large red onion, peeled and thinly sliced
1 large green bell pepper, seeds and ribs removed, and thinly sliced
1 jalapeño or serrano chile, seeds and ribs removed, and finely chopped
2 garlic cloves, peeled and minced
2 medium ripe tomatoes, rinsed, cored, seeded, and diced
1/4 cup lime juice
2 teaspoons ground cumin
1/4 cup chopped fresh cilantro
Salt and freshly ground black pepper to taste

Adult addition:

1 additional jalapeño or serrano chile, seeds and ribs removed, and finely chopped

TO SERVE

8–12 (6-inch) flour tortillas
Sour cream
Salsa
Guacamole

1. Rinse chicken and pat dry with paper towels. Trim chicken of all visible fat, and cut into 3/4-inch slices across the grain. Cut slices into 3/4-inch strips.
2. Heat 2 tablespoons oil in a large skillet over medium-high heat. Add chicken and cook, stirring frequently, for 4–5 minutes, or until chicken is cooked through and no longer pink. Remove chicken from the skillet with a slotted spoon, set aside, and keep warm. Discard fat from the skillet, and wipe out the skillet with paper towels.

3. Heat remaining oil in the skillet over medium-high heat. Add onion, green bell pepper, chile, and garlic. Cook, stirring frequently, for 4–6 minutes, or until onion softens. Add tomato, and cook for 1 minute. Add lime juice, cumin, cilantro, and chicken, and heat through, stirring constantly. Season to taste with salt and pepper. Add additional raw chile to adult portions, if desired.
4. Wrap tortillas in plastic wrap, and microwave on high (100 percent power) for 20–30 seconds, or until warm and pliable. To serve, roll up filling in tortillas, and serve with small bowls of sour cream, salsa, and guacamole. Serve immediately.

Note: The dish can be made 2 hours in advance and kept at room temperature.

Variation:
- Substitute sirloin tips for the chicken, and cook the beef for 1½–2 minutes, or to desired doneness.

Cumin, pronounced *KOO-men,* is frequently found in markets under its Spanish name, *comino.* The seeds from which it's ground are the dried fruit from a plant in the parsley family, which is very aromatic. It's one of the major ingredients in commercial chili powder, so you can always substitute chili powder if necessary.

Mexican Chicken and Rice (*Arroz con Pollo*)

This is one of those wonderful all-in-one dishes; the rice cooks in the same savory Mexican sauce as the pieces of chicken. It's incredibly flavorful, without being overly spicy.

Yield: 4–6 servings | **Active time:** 20 minutes | **Start to finish:** 50 minutes

- 1 (3½–4-pound) frying chicken, cut into serving pieces, with each breast half cut in half crosswise
- Salt and freshly ground black pepper to taste
- 3 tablespoons olive oil
- 1 large onion, peeled and diced
- 2 garlic cloves, peeled and minced
- 1 cup long-grain white rice
- 1 (14.5-ounce) can diced tomatoes, drained
- 1 (4-ounce) can diced mild green chiles, drained
- 1¾ cups Chicken Stock (recipe on page 55) or purchased stock
- 2 teaspoons ground cumin
- 1 teaspoon dried oregano
- 1 bay leaf
- 1 (10-ounce) package frozen corn kernels, thawed

Adult addition:
- ½ cup sliced pimiento-stuffed green olives

1. Rinse chicken, pat dry with paper towels, and sprinkle with salt and pepper. Heat oil in a large skillet over medium-high heat. Add chicken pieces to the pan, and brown well on all sides, turning gently with tongs, and being careful not to crowd the pan. Remove chicken from the pan, and set aside.

2. Add onion and garlic to the pan, and cook, stirring frequently, for 3 minutes, or until onion is translucent. Add rice to the pan, and cook for 1 minute, stirring constantly. Add tomatoes, chiles, stock, cumin, oregano, and bay leaf to the pan, and bring to a boil over high heat, stirring frequently.

3. Return chicken to the pan, cover the pan, reduce the heat to medium-low, and cook for 25–35 minutes, or until chicken is cooked through and no longer pink, and almost all liquid has been absorbed.

4. Stir in corn, re-cover the pan, and cook for 2–3 minutes, or until hot and remaining liquid is absorbed. Remove and discard bay leaf, season to taste with salt and pepper, and serve immediately. Add olives to adult portions, if desired.

Note: The dish can be cooked up to 2 days in advance and refrigerated, tightly covered. Reheat in a 350°F oven, covered, for 20–25 minutes, or until hot.

Variation:
- Substitute 1 (15-ounce) can red kidney beans, drained and rinsed, for the corn.

There are two types of chiles in small cans in the Hispanic food section of supermarkets. What is specified here are the mild green chiles, but the small cans of fiery jalapeño peppers look very similar. Look at the cans carefully; not only would jalapeño peppers waste your money, they would ruin this dish.

Turkey Chili

Making traditional chili with lean and inexpensive ground turkey has been becoming more common in the past few years, and I adore it. The addition of a bit of cocoa powder adds a depth of flavor to the dish.

Yield: 4–6 servings | **Active time:** 15 minutes | **Start to finish:** 45 minutes

> 2 tablespoons olive oil
> 1 medium onion, peeled and diced
> 2 garlic cloves, peeled and minced
> 1 small green bell pepper, seeds and ribs removed, and chopped
> 1 pound ground turkey
> 2 tablespoons all-purpose flour
> 2 tablespoons chili powder
> 1 tablespoon ground cumin
> 1 teaspoon dried oregano
> 2 teaspoons unsweetened cocoa powder
> 1 (28-ounce) can diced tomatoes, undrained
> 2 (15-ounce) cans kidney beans, drained and rinsed
> Salt and freshly ground black pepper to taste

Adult addition:
> 1–2 chipotle chiles in adobo sauce, finely chopped

1. Heat oil in a saucepan over medium-high heat. Add onion, garlic, and green bell pepper. Cook, stirring frequently, for 3 minutes, or until onion is translucent. Add turkey and cook, stirring constantly, for 5 minutes, breaking up lumps with a fork.

2. Stir in flour, chili powder, cumin, oregano, and cocoa. Cook over low heat, stirring frequently, for 2 minutes. Add tomatoes and bring to a boil over medium heat. Simmer chili, partially covered and stirring occasionally, for 25 minutes, or until thick. Add beans, and cook for an additional 5 minutes. Season to taste with salt and pepper, and add chipotle chiles to adult portions, if desired.

Note: The dish can be prepared up to 2 days in advance and refrigerated, tightly covered. Reheat it, covered, in a saucepan over low heat.

Variations:
- Substitute ground beef or ground pork for the turkey.
- There's a related dish in Mexican cooking called *picadillo.* Omit the oregano, and add 1/2 teaspoon ground cinnamon, 1/2 cup raisins, and 1 tablespoon cider vinegar to the chili.

Any chili can become a finger food by being turned into nachos. Pile the chili on large nacho corn chips, top with some grated Monterey Jack cheese, and pop under the broiler until the cheese is melted.

Easy Beef Tacos

Now, you know this will be a hit when you put it in front of the kids! And when tacos are made with fresh ingredients, they leave the realm of fast food and become healthful, fun food.

Yield: 4–6 servings | **Active time:** 15 minutes | **Start to finish:** 30 minutes

BEEF FILLING

3 tablespoons olive oil, divided
³/₄ pound lean ground beef
1 small onion, peeled and chopped
2 garlic cloves, peeled and minced
1 tablespoon chili powder
1 tablespoon smoked Spanish paprika
1 teaspoon ground cumin
1 teaspoon dried oregano
1 (8-ounce) can tomato sauce
2 teaspoons firmly packed light brown sugar
2 teaspoons cider vinegar
Salt and freshly ground black pepper to taste

Adult addition:
Hot red pepper sauce to taste

TO SERVE

8–12 taco shells, made according to the directions given on page
   113 or purchased and heated according to package directions
1 cup shredded iceberg lettuce
2–3 ripe plum tomatoes, rinsed, cored, seeded, and chopped
¹/₂–³/₄ cup grated cheddar or Monterey Jack cheese

1. Heat 1 tablespoon oil in a large skillet over medium-high heat. Add beef, breaking up lumps with a fork, and brown well. Remove beef from the skillet with a slotted spoon, discard grease, and set aside.

2. Heat remaining oil in the skillet, and add onion and garlic. Cook, stirring frequently, for 3 minutes, or until onion is translucent. Stir in chili powder, paprika, cumin, and oregano, and cook for 1 minute, stirring constantly.

3. Return beef to the skillet, add tomato sauce, brown sugar, and vinegar. Bring to a boil, reduce the heat to low, and simmer, uncovered, for 10–12 minutes, or until thickened, stirring frequently. Season to taste with salt and pepper. Season adult portions with hot red pepper sauce, if desired.

4. To serve, place a portion of beef filling in the bottom of each taco shell, and top with lettuce, tomato, and cheese. Serve immediately.

Note: The beef filling can be prepared up to 2 days in advance and refrigerated, tightly covered. Reheat it over low heat, covered, until hot, stirring occasionally.

Variations:
- Substitute ground turkey for the ground beef.

> While tacos are authentically Mexican, the crisp taco shell is an American innovation, first described in a mid-twentieth-century cookbook. What we now call "soft tacos," made with flour tortillas, are the true Mexican taco.

Summer Taco Salad

Getting kids to eat a large salad can present quite a challenge, according to the parents who advised me on this book. One way around that is to include a large component of something they already like—in this case, taco filling.

Yield: 4–6 servings | **Active time:** 20 minutes | **Start to finish:** 40 minutes

BEEF

3 tablespoons olive oil, divided
1 pound ground beef
1 small red onion, peeled and chopped
2 garlic cloves, peeled and minced
1 small jalapeño or serrano chile, seeds and ribs removed, and finely chopped
1 tablespoon chili powder
1 teaspoon ground cumin
1 teaspoon dried oregano
1 (8-ounce) can tomato sauce
½ cup Beef Stock (recipe on page 56) or purchased stock
1 (15-ounce) can pinto beans, drained and rinsed
Salt and freshly ground black pepper to taste

DRESSING

¼ cup lime juice
3 tablespoons chopped fresh cilantro
1 garlic clove, peeled and minced
1 tablespoon granulated sugar
1 teaspoon dried oregano
Salt and freshly ground black pepper to taste
½ cup olive oil

SALAD

4–6 cups firmly packed shredded iceberg lettuce
2–3 ripe plum tomatoes, rinsed, cored, seeded, and chopped
1 ripe avocado, peeled and diced
1–1½ cups grated cheddar cheese
Salted corn tortilla chips

Adult additions:

½ cup sliced pimiento-stuffed green olives
2–3 scallions, white parts and 3 inches of green tops, rinsed, trimmed, and sliced

1. Heat 1 tablespoon oil in a large skillet over medium-high heat. Add beef, breaking up lumps with a fork, and cook for 3 minutes, or until browned. Remove beef from the skillet with a slotted spoon, and set aside. Discard fat from the skillet.
2. Heat remaining oil in the skillet over medium-high heat. Add onion, garlic, and chile, and cook, stirring frequently, for 3 minutes, or until onion is translucent. Add chili powder, cumin, and oregano, and cook for 1 minute, stirring constantly.
3. Return beef to the skillet, and add tomato sauce and stock. Bring to a boil, reduce the heat to low, and simmer beef, uncovered, for 10 minutes. Add beans, simmer for an additional 5 minutes, and season to taste with salt and pepper. Keep warm.
4. While beef simmers, prepare dressing. Combine lime juice, cilantro, garlic, sugar, oregano, salt, and pepper in a jar with a tight-fitting lid, and shake well. Add oil, and shake well again. Set aside.
5. Place lettuce, tomatoes, avocado, and cheese in a mixing bowl. Toss gently with dressing. Mound salad on individual plates or a serving platter. Add olives and scallions to adult portions, if desired. Layer beef on top, and serve tortilla chips alongside.

Note: The beef mixture and dressing can be prepared up to 2 days in advance and refrigerated, tightly covered. Reheat the beef over low heat, covered, until hot, and allow the dressing to sit at room temperature for 30 minutes before serving.

Variation:
- Substitute ground turkey for the ground beef.

Pork Stew with Mole Sauce

Mole is one of the oldest sauces in the New World; it dates back to the Aztec Indians of Mexico centuries before Columbus landed in America. Its most salient feature is the inclusion of some sort of bitter chocolate, which adds richness to the dark, reddish-brown sauce without adding sweetness.

Yield: 4–6 servings | **Active time:** 20 minutes | **Start to finish:** 2½ hours

- 1¼ pounds boneless pork loin, cut into 1-inch cubes
- Salt and freshly ground black pepper to taste
- 3 tablespoons olive oil
- 2 large onions, peeled and chopped
- 2 garlic cloves, peeled and minced
- 2 tablespoons chili powder
- 1 teaspoon ground cumin
- 3 cups Chicken Stock (recipe on page 55) or purchased stock
- 1 (14.5-ounce) can tomatoes, drained
- ¼ cup peanut butter
- ¼ cup chopped raisins
- 2 tablespoons granulated sugar
- 2 tablespoons unsweetened cocoa powder
- 3 carrots, peeled and cut into 1-inch pieces
- 2 large sweet potatoes, peeled and cut into 1-inch pieces
- 1 cup fresh corn kernels or frozen corn kernels, thawed

Adult addition:

- 1–2 chipotle chiles in adobo sauce, finely chopped

1. Preheat the oven to 350°F. Rinse pork and pat dry with paper towels. Sprinkle pork with salt and pepper. Heat oil in a Dutch oven over medium-high heat. Add pork, and cook, turning pieces with tongs, until brown on all sides. Remove pork from the pan with tongs, and set aside.

2. Add onions and garlic to the pan, and cook, stirring frequently, for 3 minutes, or until onions are translucent. Stir in chili powder and cumin, and cook for 1 minute, stirring constantly.

3. Add stock, tomatoes, peanut butter, raisins, sugar, and cocoa powder. Stir well, and bring to a boil over high heat. Reduce the heat to low and simmer sauce for 10 minutes, or until lightly thickened. Return pork to the pan, and add carrots and sweet potato cubes. Bring to a boil again, and transfer pan to the oven.

4. Bake stew, covered, for 1¾ hours. Add corn, and bake for an additional 15 minutes. Season to taste with salt and pepper, and serve immediately. Add chipotle chile to adult portions, if desired.

Note: The dish can be cooked up to 2 days in advance and refrigerated, tightly covered. Reheat, covered, in a 350°F oven for 25–30 minutes, or until hot.

Variation:

- Substitute 1 (3½–4-pound) frying chicken, cut into serving pieces, with each breast half cut in half crosswise, for the pork. The cooking time will remain the same.

The Aztec Indians equated cocoa powder, which they termed "food of the gods" with great achievement. It's said that the leaders would drink multiple glasses a day of what we now call hot cocoa.

New Mexican Pork and Hominy Stew (*Pozole*)

Corn is the quintessentially American food, and it was raised by Native American tribes from the Atlantic to the Pacific. This dish is relatively quick to make because it uses canned hominy, so soaking the kernels is not necessary.

Yield: 4–6 servings | **Active time:** 15 minutes | **Start to finish:** 2½ hours

STEW

1¼ pounds boneless pork loin, cut into 1-inch cubes

Salt and freshly ground black pepper to taste

2 tablespoons olive oil

1 large onion, peeled and diced

2 garlic cloves, peeled and minced

1 small jalapeño or serrano chile, seeds and ribs removed, and finely chopped

2 tablespoons chili powder

2 teaspoon ground cumin

1½ cups Chicken Stock (recipe on page 55) or purchased stock

1 (14.5-ounce) can diced tomatoes, undrained

2 (15-ounce) cans yellow hominy, drained and rinsed well

1 cup fresh or frozen corn kernels, thawed

GARNISH

Sour cream

Lime wedges

1. Preheat the oven to 350°F. Rinse pork and pat dry with paper towels. Sprinkle pork with salt and pepper. Heat oil in a Dutch oven over medium-high heat. Add pork, and cook, turning pieces with tongs, until brown on all sides. Remove pork from the pan with tongs, and set aside.

2. Add onion, garlic, and chile to the pan, and cook, stirring frequently, for 3 minutes, or until onion is translucent. Stir in chili powder and cumin, and cook, stirring constantly, for 1 minute. Return meat to pan, and stir in stock and tomatoes. Bring to a boil over medium-high

heat. Cover the pan, and bake for 1 hour. Add hominy and corn, and bake for 1 hour, or until pork is very tender. Serve immediately, passing bowls of sour cream and lime wedges.

Note: The dish can be cooked up to 2 days in advance and refrigerated, tightly covered. Reheat, covered, in a 350°F oven for 25–30 minutes, or until hot.

Variation:
- Substitute 1 (3½–4-pound) frying chicken, cut into serving pieces, with each breast half cut in half crosswise, for the pork. Reduce the initial baking time to 30 minutes before adding the hominy.

> Pork is much more delicate in flavor and lighter in color than beef or lamb, so the stock that should be used for pork dishes is chicken rather than beef. Pork is rarely, if ever, made into a stock of its own, although smoked ham bones can be used to flavor stocks and soups.

Chapter 7:
Mediterranean Madness

Twirling pasta on a fork is second only to food you pick up in your hands as a fun meal in kids' minds. And there's a lot more than spaghetti and meatballs.

In recent years not only Italian food but the cuisines of other countries bordering the Mediterranean Sea have been justly touted for promoting good health. The use of olive oil instead of butter, few high-fat dairy products, a large proportion of vegetables to protein—including healthful and inexpensive beans—are all factors cited as important to health.

In this chapter you'll find a wide selection of recipes from those countries, including the sunny flavors from Provençal France as well as from Greece and North Africa. These meals can become history lessons, too. Brush up on your Greek and Roman Empire history and mythology. There are some great stories to be told.

THE PASTA PARADE

Good-quality dried pasta is made with a high percentage of high-gluten semolina, the inner part of the grain of hard durum wheat. The gluten gives the pasta resilience, and allows it to cook while remaining somewhat firm, the elusive al dente quality.

Many pasta recipes are written for a specific shape of pasta; however, there is wide latitude for substitution. What's important is to find a pasta of about the same dimensions that cooks in the same amount of time. Those are your guides to matching a shape with a sauce. If you're trying to use whole wheat pasta to reduce the amount of refined carbs in your diet, there aren't as many shapes available. That's where the chart on pages 139–140 can come in handy.

The times given in the chart should be used as guidance, but the best way to cook pasta is according to the times listed on the individual box; each manufacturer has a slightly different formula and tests its pasta for timing.

Following are the most common types of dried pasta.

Name	(Meaning)	Description	Cooking Time
Anelli	(Rings)	Medium, ridged tubes cut into thin rings	6–8 minutes
Cannelloni	(Large Pipes)	Large cylinders	8–10 minutes with further baking
Capellini	(Hair)	Thinnest strands	2–4 minutes
Cavatappi	(Corkscrews)	Short ridged pasta twisted into a spiral	8–10 minutes
Conchiglie	(Shells)	Shells about 1 inch long	8–10 minutes
Ditalini	(Little Thimbles)	Very short round pieces	6–9 minutes
Farfalle	(Butterflies)	Flat rectangles pinched in the center to form a bow	10–12 minutes
Fettuccine	(Little Ribbons)	Long, flat ribbon shapes, about $1/4$ inch wide	6–9 minutes
Fusilli	(Twisted Spaghetti)	Long, spring-shaped strands	10–12 minutes
Gemilli	(Twins)	Medium strands woven together and cut into 2-inch lengths	8–10 minutes
Linguine	(Little Tongues)	Thin, slightly flattened solid strands about $1/8$ inch wide	6–9 minutes
Maccheroni	(Macaroni)	Thin, tubular pasta in various widths	8–10 minutes
Manicotti	(Small Muffs)	Thick, ridged tubes	10–12 minutes
Mostaccioli	(Small Mustaches)	Medium-size tubes with angle-cut ends	8–10 minutes
Orecchiette	(Ears)	Smooth, curved rounds about $1/2$ inch in diameter	6–9 minutes
Orzo	(Barley)	Tiny, rice-shaped pasta	6–9 minutes

Name	(Meaning)	Description	Cooking Time
Penne	(Quills)	Small tubes with angle-cut ends	8–10 minutes
Radiatore	(Radiators)	Short, thick, and ruffled	8–10 minutes
Rigatoni	(Large Grooved)	Thick, ridged tubes about 1½ inches long	10–12 minutes
Riso	(Rice)	Tiny grains	4–6 minutes
Rotelle	(Wheels)	Spiral-shaped with spokes	8–10 minutes
Rotini	(Spirals)	Two thick strands twisted	8–10 minutes
Spaghetti	(Length of Cord)	Thin, long strands	8–10 minutes
Vermicelli	(Little Worms)	Thinner than spaghetti	6–8 minutes
Ziti	(Bridegroom)	Medium-size tubes about about 2 inches long	10–12 minutes

Pasta with Zucchini

This is such a quick and easy recipe, my guess is that you'll make it a part of your repertoire. Nutritious and inexpensive zucchini is cut into thin ribbons that blend in with the pasta strands.

Yield: 4-6 servings | **Active time:** 20 minutes | **Start to finish:** 20 minutes

2/3 pound spaghetti
4 small zucchini
3 tablespoons unsalted butter
3 tablespoons olive oil
3 garlic cloves, peeled and minced
2 teaspoons dried basil
1/2 cup freshly grated Parmesan cheese
Salt and freshly ground black pepper to taste

Adult addition:
1/4-1/2 teaspoon crushed red pepper flakes

1. Bring a large pot of salted water to a boil. Add pasta, and cook according to package directions until al dente. Drain, reserving 1 cup of pasta cooking water. Return pasta to the pan.

2. While water heats, rinse and trim zucchini. Cut zucchini lengthwise into 1/2-inch-thick slices. Stack slices, and cut into 1/2-inch-thick strips.

3. Heat butter and oil in a large skillet over medium heat. Add zucchini, garlic, and basil, and cook, stirring frequently, for 6-8 minutes, or until zucchini softens. Add zucchini mixture to the pan with pasta, and toss with cheese, salt, and pepper. Add reserved pasta cooking liquid a few tablespoons at a time until proper moisture level is reached. Serve immediately. Add crushed red pepper flakes to adult portions, if desired.

Note: The zucchini can be prepared up to 1 day in advance and refrigerated, tightly covered. Reheat it over low heat, covered, until hot.

Variation:
• Substitute yellow squash for some or all of the zucchini.

Pasta Shells Stuffed with Spinach and Ricotta

Kids love the shape of shell pasta; eating them becomes a game because the filling is hidden. In this case the filling is creamy ricotta cheese and bright green spinach. Serve it with a tossed salad.

Yield: 4–6 servings | **Active time:** 20 minutes | **Start to finish:** 50 minutes

12–18 large pasta shells
1 (10-ounce) package frozen chopped spinach, thawed
2 tablespoons olive oil
1 medium onion, peeled and chopped
1 garlic clove, peeled and minced
1 cup ricotta cheese
1 cup freshly grated Parmesan cheese, divided
2 tablespoons chopped fresh parsley
1 teaspoon Italian seasoning
Salt and freshly ground black pepper to taste
2 cups Herbed Tomato Sauce (recipe on page 32) or purchased
    marinara sauce
$1/2$ cup grated whole-milk mozzarella cheese

Adult additions:

$1/4$–$1/2$ teaspoon crushed red pepper flakes
1–2 additional garlic cloves, peeled and minced

1. Preheat the oven to 350°F, and grease a 9 x 13-inch baking pan. Bring a large pot of salted water to a boil over high heat. Cook shells according to package directions until al dente. Drain, and set aside. Place spinach in a colander, and press with the back of a spoon to extract as much liquid as possible. Place spinach in a large mixing bowl.

2. Heat oil in a small skillet over medium-high heat. Add onion and garlic, and cook, stirring frequently, for 5 minutes, or until onion softens. Scrape onion into the mixing bowl, and add ricotta, $1/2$ cup Parmesan, parsley, Italian seasoning, salt, and pepper. Mix well. Add crushed red pepper flakes and additional garlic to adult portions, if desired.

3. Place $1/2$ cup tomato sauce on the bottom of the prepared pan. Stuff cooked shells with spinach filling, and arrange them on top of sauce with their filling facing up. Top with remaining sauce, remaining Parmesan, and mozzarella cheese.

4. Cover the pan with foil, and bake for 15 minutes. Remove the foil, and bake for an additional 15–20 minutes, or until cheese melts and sauce is bubbly. Serve immediately.

Note: The dish can be prepared up to 2 days in advance and refrigerated, tightly covered. Reheat it, covered, in a 350°F oven for 20–25 minutes, or until hot.

Variations:
- Substitute chopped broccoli, cooked according to package directions and well drained, for the spinach.
- Substitute 1 cup chopped cooked chicken for ½ of the spinach.

The short baking time of a dish such as this one means that the filling has to be fully cooked in advance; it will merely heat well in the sauce.

Creamy Polenta

Cooking polenta—basically a cornmeal mush—used to demand that the cook had great biceps; it needed almost constant stirring for a long period of time. This method, however, cooks the polenta covered, so stirring is reduced. I'm including this recipe because it can be used as an alternative to pasta to top with a favorite sauce.

Yield: 4–6 servings | **Active time:** 10 minutes | **Start to finish:** 45 minutes

> 3 cups water
> 1 cup whole milk
> 1 teaspoon salt
> 1 cup polenta
> 2 tablespoons unsalted butter, cut into small bits
> Salt and freshly ground black pepper to taste

1. Bring water, milk, and salt to a boil in a 3-quart saucepan over high heat. Whisk in polenta in a thin stream, whisking so no lumps form.
2. Reduce the heat to medium, and continue to whisk for 2 minutes. Cover the pan, reduce the heat to the lowest setting, and stir with a heavy spoon every 8–10 minutes for 30 seconds, or until polenta is smooth again. Continue to cook for 30 minutes.
3. Remove the pan from the heat, and stir in butter. Season to taste with pepper, and additional salt, if necessary. Serve immediately.

Note: The dish can be prepared up to 20 minutes in advance. If holding it for longer than that time, add additional milk and butter to create a creamy consistency again.

Variations:
- Substitute Chicken Stock (recipe on page 55) or Vegetable Stock (page 57) for the water.
- Add 2 tablespoons chopped fresh parsley and ½ teaspoon Italian seasoning to the water.
- Add ½–¾ cup grated whole-milk mozzarella cheese, a combination of whole-milk mozzarella and freshly grated Parmesan cheese, or Swiss cheese along with the butter.

- For crispy polenta, make the recipe above, and pack it into a well-greased 9 x 5 x 3-inch loaf pan. Chill well. Unmold the loaf, and cut into 1-inch slices. Cut each slice into 2 triangles. Heat 3 tablespoons olive oil in a large skillet over medium-high heat. Add polenta triangles, and cook for 2–3 minutes per side, or until browned and crisp, turning triangles gently with a spatula.

Polenta is a coarse yellow cornmeal. If you want to use regular yellow cornmeal for this dish, it will cook in 20 minutes.

Spiced Couscous with Vegetables

Couscous, a tiny granular pasta used in North African cooking, has become very popular in this country in recent years. In this case it's topped with a colorful and flavorful mélange of spiced vegetables.

Yield: 4–6 servings | **Active time:** 15 minutes | **Start to finish:** 1¾ hours

STOCK

- 4 cups Vegetable Stock (recipe on page 57) or purchased stock
- 2 tablespoons olive oil
- 4 large fresh cilantro sprigs, rinsed
- 3 garlic cloves, peeled
- 2 (3-inch) cinnamon sticks
- 2 teaspoons curry powder
- 2 teaspoons ground cumin
- 2 teaspoons paprika

DISH

- 3 medium carrots, peeled, halved lengthwise, and cut into 1-inch pieces
- 2 Idaho potatoes, peeled and cut into eighths
- 1 medium turnip, peeled and cut into 1-inch pieces
- 6 small onions, peeled and halved
- 2 medium zucchini, rinsed, trimmed, halved lengthwise, and cut into 1-inch lengths
- 1 (14.5-ounce) can diced tomatoes, drained
- 1 (15-ounce) can garbanzo beans, drained and rinsed
- ⅔ cup pitted prunes, halved
- Salt and freshly ground black pepper to taste
- 4–6 cups cooked couscous, prepared according to package directions, hot

1. Combine stock, oil, cilantro sprigs, garlic, cinnamon sticks, curry powder, cumin, and paprika in a Dutch oven. Bring to a boil over high heat, reduce the heat to low, and simmer, uncovered, for 20 minutes. Strain stock, discarding solids, and return stock to the pan.
2. Add carrots, potatoes, turnip, and onions to stock. Bring to a boil, reduce the heat to low, and simmer, uncovered, for 30 minutes.

3. Add zucchini, tomatoes, garbanzo beans, and prunes. Simmer, uncovered, an additional 30 minutes. Season to taste with salt and pepper. Spoon couscous into shallow bowls, and top with the vegetables and broth.

Note: The dish can be prepared up to 2 days in advance and refrigerated, tightly covered. Reheat it over low heat, covered, until simmering before serving.

Variation:
- Substitute dried apricots for the prunes.

According to my Parents Panel, adding fruit to a dish is a great way to get kids to eat it—even at a young age. Part of the reason might be that the sweet taste buds are the first ones that mature in a child.

Moroccan Fish with Carrots

Most Moroccan fish specialties are prepared with a marinade called *charmoula*. Paprika, cumin, cilantro, and garlic usually form its base, and it adds a subtle flavor to dishes. Because this dish contains carrots, there's a good chance your kids will like it.

Yield: 4–6 servings | **Active time:** 20 minutes | **Start to finish:** 3 hours, including 2 hours for marinating

> 1–1¼ pounds thick white-fleshed fish fillets
> ½ cup olive oil, divided
> 3 tablespoons chopped fresh parsley
> 3 tablespoons chopped fresh cilantro
> 2 garlic cloves, peeled and minced
> 2 teaspoons paprika
> Salt and freshly ground black pepper to taste
> 1 medium onion, peeled and chopped
> 1 pound carrots, peeled and thinly sliced
> 1 (14.5-ounce) can diced tomatoes, undrained
> 2 tablespoons lemon juice
> Vegetable oil spray

Adult addition:
> ½ cup pitted kalamata olives

1. Rinse fish and pat dry with paper towels. Cut fish into 2-inch cubes.
2. Combine ⅓ cup olive oil, parsley, cilantro, garlic, paprika, salt, and pepper in a heavy resealable plastic bag. Add fish cubes, and coat evenly with mixture. Marinate fish, refrigerated, for 2 hours.
3. Preheat the oven to 400°F, and grease a 9 x 13-inch baking dish.
4. Heat remaining oil in a skillet over medium-high heat. Add onion and carrots, and cook, stirring frequently, for 3 minutes, or until onion is translucent. Scrape mixture into the prepared pan, and add tomatoes and lemon juice. Cover the pan with foil, and bake for 20 minutes.
5. Add fish and its marinade to the pan, spooning some carrots and tomatoes on top of fish cubes. Cover the pan again, and bake for 20–25 minutes, or until fish is cooked through and flakes easily. Season to taste with salt and pepper, and serve immediately. Add olives to adult portions, if desired.

Note: The dish can be cooked up to 1 day in advance and refrigerated, tightly covered. Reheat, covered with foil, in a 350°F oven for 25–30 minutes, or until hot.

Variation:

- Substitute 1-inch cubes of boneless, skinless chicken breast for the fish, and add the chicken after the vegetables have cooked for 10 minutes.

If you have just a single carrot to peel, then the time-honored way of using a vegetable peeler makes sense. But for a whole pound there's an easier way: Cover the carrots with boiling water and allow them to sit for 3 minutes. Drain them, and run them under cold water. The peels will slip right off.

Linguine with White Clam Sauce

Pre-minced fresh clams are one of the great convenience foods on the market because they are so easy to use and so economical; it would be far more expensive to buy the number of clams that go into a pint and shuck them yourself, plus it would take a lot of time! One pint can serve a number of people when turned into this robust sauce that is a classic of northern Italian cooking.

Yield: 4–6 servings | **Active time:** 15 minutes | **Start to finish:** 35 minutes

⅔ pound linguine
1 pint fresh minced clams
¼ cup olive oil
1 small onion, peeled and chopped
2 garlic cloves, peeled and minced
1 (8-ounce) bottle clam juice
¾ cup dry white wine
¼ cup chopped fresh parsley
2 teaspoons Italian seasoning
2 ripe plum tomatoes, rinsed, cored, seeded, and diced
Salt and freshly ground black pepper to taste
½ cup freshly grated Parmesan cheese

Adult additions:
¼–½ teaspoon crushed red pepper flakes or to taste
1–2 additional garlic cloves, peeled and minced

1. Bring a large pot of salted water to a boil. Add pasta, and cook according to package directions until al dente. Drain, and set aside. Place clams in a colander over a mixing bowl. Press with the back of a spoon to extract as much liquid as possible. Refrigerate clams if not proceeding immediately.

2. Heat olive oil in a heavy saucepan over medium-high heat. Add onion and garlic and cook, stirring frequently, for 3 minutes, or until onion is translucent. Add reserved clam juice, bottled clam juice, wine, parsley, and Italian seasoning. Bring to a boil, stirring occasionally. Reduce the heat to low, and simmer sauce, uncovered, for 20 minutes, or until reduced by ½.

3. Add tomatoes and clams to sauce. Bring to a boil, and simmer for 5 minutes, stirring occasionally. Season to taste with salt and pepper. Add pasta to sauce, and serve immediately. Add red pepper flakes to adult portions, if desired. Pass Parmesan cheese separately.

Note: The sauce can be prepared up to 2 days in advance and refrigerated, tightly covered. Reheat it over low heat, and cook the pasta just prior to serving.

Variation:

- While white wine is typically used with fish, you can also use red wine if you have it around.
- Substitute ³/₄ pound firm-fleshed white fish, such as tilapia or cod, cut into ³/₄-inch cubes, for the clams.

Foods like clams cook so quickly that they should always be added to dishes at the end of cooking time; however, a sauce should not be seasoned until after they're cooked because they will give off liquid into the food.

Chicken with Lentils

Lentils are one of the few legumes that require no presoaking, so this dinner flavored with Moroccan seasonings can be on the table in a matter of minutes. Serve it over couscous.

Yield: 4–6 servings | **Active time:** 20 minutes | **Start to finish:** 40 minutes

> 1¼ pounds boneless, skinless chicken breast halves
> ½ pound brown lentils, rinsed well
> 4 cups water
> Salt and freshly ground black pepper to taste
> ¼ cup red wine vinegar
> 2 tablespoons chili powder, divided
> 1 tablespoon ground cumin, divided
> ½ cup olive oil, divided
> 1 medium onion, peeled and chopped
> 2 garlic cloves, peeled and minced
> ¼ teaspoon ground cinnamon
> ¼ cup chopped fresh parsley

1. Rinse chicken and pat dry with paper towels. Trim chicken of all visible fat, and cut into ¾-inch cubes, and set aside. Combine lentils and water in a saucepan, and season to taste with salt and pepper. Cover the pan, and bring to a boil over high heat. Reduce the heat to low, and simmer lentils for 20 minutes, or until tender. Drain, and return lentils to the pan to keep warm.
2. While lentils cook, combine vinegar, 1 tablespoon chili powder, 1 teaspoon cumin, salt, and pepper in a jar with a tight-fitting lid, and shake well. Add ⅓ cup oil, and shake well again. Set aside.
3. Heat remaining oil in a skillet over medium-high heat. Add onion and garlic, and cook for 3 minutes, or until onion is translucent. Add chicken, and sprinkle chicken with remaining chili powder, remaining cumin, and cinnamon. Cook, stirring constantly, for 5 minutes, or until chicken is cooked through and no longer pink. Season to taste with salt and pepper, and stir chicken mixture and parsley into the pan with lentils. Drizzle dressing over all, and serve immediately.

Note: The dish can be cooked up to 2 days in advance and refrigerated, tightly covered. Reheat, covered with foil, in a 350°F oven for 25–30 minutes, or until hot.

Variation:
- Substitute thick white-fleshed fish fillets, cut into 1-inch cubes, for the chicken.

The use of cumin makes many North African dishes similar in flavor to Hispanic food. Introducing foods like lentils to kids that way makes them seem far more like old friends.

Provençal Chicken

The French region of Provence also borders the Mediterranean Sea, and it is known for its sunny bright flavors and use of ingredients such as the region's famed olives. Serve this over rice, with a tossed salad on the side.

Yield: 4–6 servings | **Active time:** 20 minutes | **Start to finish:** 1¼ hours

  1 orange
  1 (3½–4-pound) frying chicken, cut into serving pieces with each breast cut in half crosswise
  Salt and freshly ground black pepper to taste
  ½ cup all-purpose flour
  ½ cup olive oil, divided
  1 medium onion, peeled and chopped
  2 garlic cloves, peeled and minced
  1 (14.5-ounce) can diced tomatoes, undrained
  1 cup Chicken Stock (recipe on page 55) or purchased stock
  ½ cup dry white wine
  2 celery ribs, rinsed, trimmed, and diced
  1 carrot, peeled and sliced
  2 tablespoons chopped fresh parsley
  1½ teaspoons herbes de Provence
  1 bay leaf
  2–3 cups cooked rice, hot

Adult addition:

  ½ cup pitted oil-cured black olives

1. Preheat the oven to 375°F. Grate zest from orange, and then squeeze juice out of fruit. Set aside.
2. Rinse chicken and pat dry with paper towels. Sprinkle chicken with salt and pepper, and dust with flour, shaking off any excess. Heat ⅓ cup oil in a Dutch oven over medium-high heat. Add chicken pieces, skin side down, being careful not to crowd the pan. Brown chicken on both sides, turning pieces gently with tongs. Remove chicken from the pan, and set aside. Discard grease from the pan.

3. Heat remaining oil in the Dutch oven over medium-high heat. Add onion and garlic, and cook, stirring frequently, for 3 minutes, or until onion is translucent. Add orange juice, orange zest, tomatoes, stock, wine, celery, carrot, parsley, herbes de Provence, and bay leaf to the pan, and bring to a boil over high heat.

4. Return chicken to the pan, and bring back to a boil. Cover the pan, and bake chicken for 45–50 minutes, or until chicken registers 165°F on an instant-read thermometer, and is cooked through and no longer pink. Remove and discard bay leaf. Season to taste with salt and pepper, and serve immediately. Add olives to adult portions, if desired.

Note: The dish can be cooked up to 2 days in advance and refrigerated, tightly covered. Reheat, covered with foil, in a 350°F oven for 25–30 minutes, or until hot.

Variation:
- Substitute pork chops for the chicken.

It's important not to crowd a pan full of food when browning it because the food gives off moisture as it cooks. The food will steam and not brown if placed too closely together.

Moroccan Chicken with Apricots

Mediterranean cooking involves a lot of dried fruits; it's one of the hallmarks of Sicilian dishes as well as those from North Africa. Succulent dried apricots are cooked with spices and then added to this kid-pleasing dish. Serve it with couscous to enjoy all the sauce.

Yield: 4–6 servings | **Active time:** 20 minutes | **Start to finish:** 1¼ hours

   1 (3½–4-pound) frying chicken, cut into serving pieces with each
      breast cut in half crosswise
   Salt and freshly ground black pepper to taste
   ½ cup all-purpose flour
   ½ cup olive oil, divided
   1 medium onion, peeled and diced
   2 garlic cloves, peeled and minced
   ¾ teaspoon ground cinnamon
   ¾ teaspoon ground ginger
   ½ teaspoon ground coriander
   1½ cups Chicken Stock (recipe on page 55) or purchased stock
   3 tablespoons chopped fresh parsley
   3 tablespoons chopped fresh cilantro (or additional parsley)
   1 cup water
   2 tablespoons honey
   1 (3-inch) cinnamon stick
   ⅔ cup chopped dried apricots

Adult addition:
   Hot red pepper sauce to taste

1. Preheat the oven to 375°F. Rinse chicken and pat dry with paper towels. Sprinkle chicken with salt and pepper, and dust with flour, shaking off any excess. Heat ⅓ cup oil in a Dutch oven over medium-high heat. Add chicken pieces, skin side down, being careful not to crowd the pan. Brown chicken on both sides, turning pieces gently with tongs. Remove chicken from the pan, and set aside. Discard grease from the pan.

2. Heat remaining oil in the Dutch oven over medium-high heat. Add onion and garlic, and cook, stirring frequently, for 3 minutes, or until onion is translucent. Stir in cinnamon, ginger, and coriander, and cook for 30 seconds, stirring constantly. Add stock, parsley, and cilantro, and stir well.

3. Return chicken to the pan, and bring back to a boil. Cover the pan, and bake chicken for 45–50 minutes, or until chicken registers 165°F on an instant-read thermometer, and is cooked through and no longer pink.

4. While chicken cooks, combine water, honey, cinnamon stick, and apricots in a small saucepan. Bring to a boil over high heat, then reduce the heat to low and cook, uncovered, for 12–15 minutes, or until apricots are very soft and liquid is syrupy. Remove and discard cinnamon stick, and add apricot mixture to chicken. Season to taste with salt and pepper, and serve immediately. Season adult portions with hot red pepper sauce, if desired.

Note: The dish can be cooked up to 2 days in advance and refrigerated, tightly covered. Reheat, covered with foil, in a 350°F oven for 25–30 minutes, or until hot.

Variation:
- Substitute pork chops for the chicken.

Chicken Scaloppine with Mushrooms

This fast and easy meal is an adaptation of a classic Italian recipe made with veal. Chicken has the same delicacy—at a fraction of the cost. It's breaded with crumbs, seasoned with herbs and cheese, and then topped with sautéed mushrooms.

Yield: 4–6 servings | **Active time:** 25 minutes | **Start to finish:** 25 minutes

1¼ pounds boneless, skinless chicken breast halves
Salt and freshly ground black pepper to taste
2 large eggs
2 cups Italian breadcrumbs
⅓ cup freshly grated Parmesan cheese
2 teaspoons Italian seasoning
½ cup olive oil, divided
3 tablespoons unsalted butter
1 small onion, peeled and chopped
2 garlic cloves, peeled and minced
½ pound mushrooms, wiped with a damp paper towel, trimmed, and sliced
⅓ cup lemon juice
2 tablespoons chopped fresh parsley

1. Preheat the oven to 150°F, and line a baking sheet with aluminum foil. Rinse chicken and pat dry with paper towels. Pound chicken between 2 sheets of plastic wrap to an even thickness of ¼ inch. Sprinkle with salt and pepper.

2. Beat eggs with a fork in a shallow bowl. Combine breadcrumbs, cheese, and Italian seasoning in another shallow bowl. Dip chicken into egg, letting any excess drip off back into the bowl, then dip meat into crumb mixture, pressing crumbs into meat on both sides.

3. Heat ⅓ cup olive oil in a large skillet over medium-high heat. Cook chicken for 2 minutes per side, or until chicken is cooked through and no longer pink. Drain chicken on paper towels. Transfer chicken to the baking sheet, and place it in the oven to keep warm.

4. Discard oil from the skillet, and wipe it with paper towels. Heat remaining olive oil and butter over medium-high heat. Add onion and garlic, and cook, stirring frequently, for 3 minutes, or until onion is translucent. Add mushrooms and cook, stirring frequently, for 5–7 minutes, or until mushrooms are lightly browned and most of liquid has evaporated. Stir in lemon juice and parsley, and season to taste with salt and pepper.
5. Remove chicken from the oven. Spoon mushrooms over chicken, and serve immediately.

Note: The chicken can be prepared up to frying up to 6 hours in advance and refrigerated, tightly covered. The mushroom mixture can be made 1 day in advance and refrigerated, tightly covered. Reheat the mushrooms over medium heat, stirring occasionally.

Variation:
- Substitute boneless pork loin, cut into 1/4-inch-thick slices, for the chicken. The pork slices should be cooked for 1 1/2–2 minutes per side.

This recipe is a great example of cooking one dish for the whole family, despite differing tastes. If there's no way that you can coax the young ones to try a mushroom, then serve the chicken to them plain.

Chicken and Pasta Primavera

Spaghetti dotted with nuggets of chicken and a cornucopia of colorful fresh vegetables in a creamy sauce laced with cheese is a nutritious as well as delicious dish.

Yield: 4–6 servings | **Active time:** 20 minutes | **Start to finish:** 25 minutes

- ²/₃ pound thin spaghetti
- ¹/₃ cup olive oil, divided
- ³/₄ pound boneless, skinless chicken breast halves
- 1 small onion, peeled and finely chopped
- 2 garlic cloves, peeled and minced
- 1 small zucchini, rinsed, trimmed, and cut into ¹/₂-inch dice
- ¹/₄ pound mushrooms, wiped with a damp paper towel, trimmed, and thinly sliced
- ¹/₂ green bell pepper, seeds and ribs removed, and sliced
- 1 (14.5-ounce) can diced tomatoes, drained
- 1 cup Chicken Stock (recipe on page 55) or purchased stock
- 1 cup heavy cream
- ¹/₄ cup chopped fresh parsley
- 2 teaspoons Italian seasoning
- 1 cup broccoli florets
- ¹/₂ cup frozen peas, thawed
- Salt and freshly ground black pepper to taste
- ³/₄ cup freshly grated Parmesan cheese

1. Bring a large pot of salted water to a boil. Add pasta, and cook according to package directions until al dente. Drain, toss with 2 tablespoons olive oil, and return pasta to the pot to keep warm.
2. Rinse chicken and pat dry with paper towels. Trim chicken of all visible fat, and cut into ³/₄-inch cubes. Heat remaining oil in a large skillet over medium-high heat. Add chicken and cook for 3 minutes, stirring frequently.
3. Add onion and garlic and cook, stirring frequently, for 3 minutes, or until onion is translucent. Add zucchini, mushrooms, and green bell pepper. Cook for 3 minutes, stirring frequently.

4. Add tomatoes, stock, cream, parsley, Italian seasoning, broccoli, and peas to the skillet. Bring to a boil over medium-high heat, and simmer, uncovered, for 3 minutes. Season to taste with salt and pepper. To serve, add drained pasta to the skillet, and toss with cheese. Serve immediately.

Note: The sauce can be prepared up to 4 hours in advance and kept at room temperature. Reheat it over low heat to a simmer before adding the pasta.

Variations:
- Substitute ³/₄ pound cooked ham, cut into ³/₄-inch dice, for the chicken. Add it to the skillet along with the liquids.
- Substitute 1 (15-ounce) can garbanzo beans, drained and rinsed, for the chicken, and substitute Vegetable Stock (recipe on page 57) for Chicken Stock.

Primavera is the Italian word for "springtime," and although this dish sounds quintessentially Italian, it was born and bred in New York. Restaurateur Sirio Maccioni created it in the mid-1970s for his famed Le Cirque restaurant, and food writers popularized the dish nationally.

Spaghetti Bolognese

What defines a true Bolognese sauce is the inclusion of both milk and white wine with the vegetables and tomatoes to make the meat in the sauce tender. You can use any pasta you choose.

Yield: 6–8 servings | **Active time:** 15 minutes | **Start to finish:** 1¼ hours

- ¼ cup olive oil, divided
- ¾ pound ground chuck
- ¾ pound ground pork
- 2 medium onions, peeled and diced
- 3 celery ribs, rinsed, trimmed, and finely chopped
- 2 carrots, peeled and finely chopped
- 2 garlic cloves, peeled and minced
- 1 (28-ounce) can diced tomatoes, undrained
- ½ cup whole milk
- ½ cup dry white wine
- ¼ cup chopped fresh parsley
- 1 tablespoon dried oregano
- 2 teaspoons dried thyme
- 1 bay leaf
- Salt and freshly ground black pepper to taste
- 1 pound spaghetti
- ½–¾ cup freshly grated Parmesan cheese

Adult addition:
- ¼–½ teaspoon crushed red pepper flakes

1. Heat 2 tablespoons olive oil in a heavy 2-quart saucepan over medium-high heat. Add beef and pork, breaking up lumps with a fork. Cook meats for 3 minutes, stirring occasionally, or until no longer pink. Remove meats from the pan with a slotted spoon, and set aside. Discard grease from the pan.

2. Heat remaining olive oil in the pan over medium-high heat. Add onions, celery, carrots, and garlic. Cook, stirring frequently, for 3 minutes, or until onions are translucent. Return meats to the pan and add tomatoes, milk, wine, parsley, oregano, thyme, and bay leaf.

3. Bring to a boil, reduce the heat to low, and simmer sauce, uncovered and stirring occasionally, for 1 hour, or until thickened. Remove and discard bay leaf, and season to taste with salt and pepper. Add crushed red pepper flakes to adult portions, if desired.

4. While sauce simmers, bring a large pot of salted water to a boil. Add pasta, and cook according to package directions until al dente. Drain pasta, and top with sauce. Serve immediately, passing Parmesan separately.

Note: The sauce can be prepared up to 3 days in advance and refrigerated, tightly covered. Reheat it over low heat, covered. The sauce can also be frozen for up to 3 months.

Variation:

- Substitute ground turkey for the ground beef and pork.

While I adore the flavor of a long-simmered sauce, if you want to speed up this recipe, cook the sauce in a deep skillet rather than a saucepan. You can cook it over medium heat for 30–40 minutes. The sauce thickens faster because the skillet has a larger surface area for evaporation.

Italian Stuffed Peppers

Stuffed vegetables fall into the category of fun food, according to the members of my Parents Panel. This ground beef stuffing is similar to a meatball, and it should be served with some pasta to enjoy all the sauce.

Yield: 4–6 servings | **Active time:** 15 minutes | **Start to finish:** 1¼ hours

- 4–6 small green bell peppers
- 2 tablespoons olive oil
- 1 large onion, peeled and chopped
- 2 garlic cloves, peeled and minced
- ¼ cup chopped fresh parsley
- 2 teaspoons Italian seasoning
- Salt and freshly ground black pepper to taste
- ¾ cup Italian breadcrumbs
- ¼ cup milk
- ½ cup grated whole-milk mozzarella cheese
- 1½ cups Herbed Tomato Sauce (recipe on page 32) or purchased marinara sauce, divided
- 2 large eggs, lightly beaten
- 1 pound lean ground beef
- ½ cup freshly grated Parmesan cheese

1. Preheat the oven to 375°F, and grease a 9 x 13-inch baking pan. Cut off top ½ inch of peppers and reserve. Scoop out and discard seeds and ribs from peppers with your hands. Discard stems, and chop flesh from reserved pepper tops.

2. Heat oil in heavy, large skillet over medium-high heat. Add onion, garlic, and chopped pepper pieces. Cook, stirring frequently, for 5–7 minutes, or until vegetables soften. Scrape mixture into a large mixing bowl.

3. Add parsley, Italian seasoning, salt, pepper, breadcrumbs, milk, mozzarella, ½ cup tomato sauce, eggs, and beef to the mixing bowl. Mix well.

4. Fill pepper cavities with beef mixture. Stand peppers up in prepared pan, and pour remaining sauce over them. Cover the pan with aluminum foil, and bake for 25 minutes. Remove the pan from the oven, baste peppers with sauce, and sprinkle with Parmesan cheese. Bake, uncovered, for an additional 20–25 minutes, or until beef is cooked through and registers 165°F on an instant-read thermometer. Serve immediately, spooning the sauce over the top of the peppers.

Note: The dish can be cooked up to 2 days in advance and refrigerated, tightly covered. Reheat, covered with foil, in a 350°F oven for 25–30 minutes, or until hot.

Variation:

- Substitute Italian sausage or ground turkey for the ground beef.

Basting is the process of brushing or spooning sauce or fat over food as it cooks. The purpose of basting is to keep food moist as well as to add flavor and color.

Greek Lamb and Eggplant (*Moussaka*)

Topped with a custard sauce, this cinnamon-scented lamb and eggplant filling is a favorite in Greek tavernas; I think of it as the Mediterranean version of Shepherd's Pie. I usually serve it with just a salad because the dish is very rich.

Yield: 6–8 servings | **Active time:** 20 minutes | **Start to finish:** 1½ hours

FILLING

1 large eggplant (1½ pounds), cap discarded, cut into ¾-inch dice
1½ pounds ground lamb
¼ cup olive oil
1 large onion, peeled and diced
3 garlic cloves, peeled and minced
1 (15-ounce) can tomato sauce
¾ cup dry red wine
2 tablespoons chopped fresh parsley
1 teaspoon dried oregano
½ teaspoon ground cinnamon
Salt and freshly ground black pepper to taste

TOPPING

4 tablespoons (½ stick) unsalted butter
¼ cup all-purpose flour
2 cups whole milk
3 large eggs, lightly beaten
¾ cup freshly grated Parmesan cheese, divided
3 tablespoons chopped fresh dill (optional)

1. Place eggplant in a mixing bowl, and cover with heavily salted water; use 1 tablespoon table salt per 1 quart water. Soak eggplant for 30 minutes, then drain and squeeze hard to remove water. Wring out remaining water with a cloth tea towel, and set aside.
2. Preheat the oven to 375°F, and grease a 9 x 13-inch baking pan.
3. Heat a large skillet over medium-high heat. Add lamb, breaking up lumps with a fork, and brown well. Remove lamb from the skillet with a slotted spoon, discard grease, and set aside.

4. Heat oil in the skillet, and add onion and garlic. Cook, stirring frequently, for 3 minutes, or until onion is translucent. Add eggplant, and cook for 3 minutes. Return lamb to the skillet, and add tomato sauce, wine, parsley, oregano, and cinnamon. Simmer for 20 minutes, stirring occasionally. Season to taste with salt and pepper.

5. While lamb simmers, prepare custard topping. Heat butter in a saucepan over low heat. Stir in flour and cook, stirring constantly, for 2 minutes. Whisk in milk, and simmer 2 minutes, or until thick. Whisk $1/2$ cup milk mixture into eggs, then whisk egg mixture back into the saucepan. Remove custard from the stove, and stir in $1/2$ cup Parmesan cheese and dill, if using. Season to taste with salt and pepper.

6. Spread meat mixture into the prepared pan. Pour hot custard topping over meat, and sprinkle with remaining $1/4$ cup Parmesan. Bake for 45 minutes, or until custard is set and top is browned. Cool 10 minutes, then serve immediately.

Note: The lamb mixture can be prepared up to 2 days in advance and refrigerated, tightly covered; reheat it over low heat before baking. Or the dish can be prepared for baking up to 6 hours in advance and kept at room temperature. Add 5–10 minutes to baking time if lamb is not hot.

Variations:
- Substitute ground beef for the lamb.
- Substitute feta cheese for the Parmesan cheese.

While it may seem like a small step, whisking some of the hot liquid into the eggs is crucial to the success of this dish, or any dish done with an egg-enriched custard. It's called "tempering" the eggs, and it makes the sauce smooth rather than like scrambled eggs.

Spaghetti with Egg and Bacon (Pasta Carbonara)

It takes longer for the water to come to a boil to cook the pasta than it does to create this classic Italian dish that's spicy with black pepper, and rich from eggs and cheese. A tossed salad is all you need to complete the meal.

Yield: 4-6 servings | **Active time:** 15 minutes | **Start to finish:** 25 minutes

> ³/₄ pound spaghetti
> ³/₄ pound bacon, sliced into ¹/₂-inch strips
> 6 garlic cloves, peeled and minced
> Freshly ground black pepper to taste
> 6 large eggs, beaten
> 1¹/₂ cups freshly grated Parmesan cheese
> Salt to taste

Adult addition:
> ¹/₂-³/₄ teaspoon additional freshly ground black pepper

1. Bring a large pot of salted water to a boil. Add pasta, and cook according to package directions until al dente. Drain, and return to the pot to keep warm.

2. While pasta boils, place bacon in a heavy 12-inch skillet over medium-high heat. Cook, stirring occasionally, for 5–7 minutes, or until crisp. Remove bacon from the skillet with a slotted spoon, and set aside. Discard all but 2 tablespoons bacon grease from the pan. Add garlic and black pepper, and cook for 30 seconds. Return bacon to the pan, and turn off heat.

3. Add drained pasta to the skillet, and cook over medium heat for 1 minute. Remove the pan from the stove, and stir in eggs. Allow eggs to thicken but do not put the pan back on the stove or they will scramble. Add cheese, and season to taste with salt and additional pepper for adult portions, if desired. Serve immediately.

Note: The bacon mixture can be cooked up to 4 hours in advance and kept at room temperature. Reheat it with pasta before adding eggs.

The last place you want your food dollars to go is to an expensive visit from the plumber, and bacon grease is notorious for clogging kitchen plumbing, even if it's put down the sink with hot water running. Rinse out empty half-pint cream containers and keep them under the sink. Pour unwanted bacon fat into a bowl, and after it cools dispose of it in the container.

Italian Sausage with Garbanzo Beans and Spinach

To make this into a healthier dish, you can substitute any uncooked chicken or turkey sausage for the pork sausage, which is higher in both fat and cholesterol. You can also make this dish spicier by using hot, rather than mild, sausage.

Yield: 4–6 servings | **Active time:** 15 minutes | **Start to finish:** 50 minutes

> 1¼ pounds sweet or hot Italian sausage links
> 1 small red onion, peeled and finely chopped
> 2 garlic cloves, peeled and minced
> 1 (10-ounce) package frozen chopped spinach, thawed
> 1 (15-ounce) can garbanzo beans, drained and rinsed
> ½ cup half-and-half
> ¾ cup freshly grated Parmesan cheese, divided
> Salt and freshly ground black pepper to taste
> ⅓ cup Italian breadcrumbs
> 2 tablespoons unsalted butter, melted

1. Preheat the oven to 375°F, and grease a 9 x 13-inch baking pan.
2. Prick sausages with the tip of a paring knife. Cook sausages over medium heat for 8–10 minutes, or until no pink remains, turning often with tongs. Drain sausages on paper towels, and slice into bite-size pieces.
3. Pour off all but 2 tablespoons of sausage fat from the skillet. Add onion and garlic and cook, stirring frequently, for 3 minutes, or until onion is translucent. Place spinach in a colander, and press with the back of a spoon to extract as much liquid as possible.
4. Combine sausage, onion mixture, spinach, beans, half-and-half, and ½ cup Parmesan in a mixing bowl. Season to taste with salt and pepper, and spread mixture into the prepared pan.
5. For topping, combine breadcrumbs, remaining Parmesan, and butter. Sprinkle on top of the casserole. Bake, covered with foil, for 15 minutes. Uncover, and bake an additional 20 minutes, or until bubbly. Serve immediately.

Note: The dish can be cooked up to 2 days in advance and refrigerated, tightly covered. Reheat, covered with foil, in a 350°F oven for 25–30 minutes, or until hot.

Variations:
- Substitute turkey sausage for the pork sausage.
- Substitute white beans for the garbanzo beans.

> When you're frying sausage links, it's your choice to fry them whole or remove them from the casings. I like to keep the casings because they hold the sausage together better, but it is important to prick them or they will burst as the liquid inside of them heats.

Chapter 8:
Pizza Power

Pizza is a great and healthful food for kids to eat as long as the dish is made with wholesome, fresh ingredients. It contains a serving of grains in the crust, dairy in the cheese, and vegetables in the tomato sauce as well as other toppings. And pizza fulfills another of the rules that make kids want to eat—they're fun to eat because you can use your hands!

You can make a pizza crust for about 50 cents, so a 12-inch pizza with lots of cheese and other toppings is less than $4. How does that compare to the cost of what you usually pay for a simple pie?

While pizza is authentically Italian, a crispy crust can serve as the base for toppings as varied as pineapple and salsa. You'll find pizza recipes reflecting a wide range of the flavor spectrum in this chapter. There are fewer actual recipes in this chapter than in most because usually when you make a pizza, you'll add toppings that appeal to your family, so there's a section for how those ingredients should be prepared prior to baking the pizza.

A note on the timing listed in the chapter: The timing of the pizza recipes was determined *after* the dough was made and patted out.

SIMPLE STEPS TO THE PERFECT PIZZA

If you know how to make pizza dough and only need to refresh your mind on the quantities of the ingredients, go right to the recipes. But if this is your first venture into turning your kitchen into a pizzeria, here is a very detailed guide to the process.

The process remains the same regardless if you like your pizza crust as thin and crispy as a cracker or as thick and chewy as a slice of bread. That aspect of the crust is determined only by how thickly or thinly you shape the dough. As you'll see, pizza dough takes time, but not effort; this is especially true if you use a food processor. Here are the steps to follow:

- **Proof the yeast.** To make sure your yeast is alive, you should start with a step called "proofing." Combine the yeast with warm liquid (100–110°F) and a small amount of flour or sugar. If the water is any hotter, it might kill the yeast. Either use a meat thermometer to take the temperature, or make sure it feels warm but not hot on the underside of your wrist. Let the mixture rest at room temperature until a thick surface foam forms, which indicates that the yeast is alive and can be used. If there is no foam, the yeast is dead and should be discarded. After your proofing is successful, you are ready to make the dough.

- **Mix the dough by hand.** Combine the flour and salt in a large mixing bowl, and make a well in the center. Add the proofed yeast, and stir with a fork in a circular motion to incorporate the flour until a jagged mass of dough forms.

- **Mix the dough in a food processor.** Use the metal blade, and add the flour and salt. With the motor running, slowly pour the yeast mixture through the feed tube. Process until the dough forms a ball.

- **Knead the dough.** This is the step that's made much faster if you use a food processor because the dough is already partially kneaded. But the method is the same, regardless of how the dough was mixed. Transfer the dough to a lightly floured counter, and push it slightly forward with the heel of your hand. Turn the ball slightly and repeat. Then fold the dough back over itself and continue to push it until the ball becomes smooth and elastic. This will take about 10 minutes if you made the dough by hand, and only 1 to 2 minutes if made in the food processor. This is a step that your kids can help you do, although it might take them a bit longer.

- **Let the dough rise.** At this juncture, your "real" work with the dough is over. Lightly grease the inside of a mixing bowl. Place the ball of dough into the bowl, and cover the bowl tightly with plastic wrap. Place the bowl in a warm room and allow it to rise until doubled in bulk. This takes 1–2 hours.

- **Punch down the dough.** This is a part of the process that kids love to do! Transfer the risen dough to a lightly floured work surface, and deflate it with the heel of your hand.

- **Shape the dough by hand.** While kids can help with this part, you'd better check to ensure an even crust. Place the punched-down dough on a lightly floured surface. Then gently stretch and lift it to shape it. For a thick crust it should be about $1/2$-inch thick, and for a crisp crust it should be about $1/4$ inch. Keep the edges slightly thicker.

- **Shape the dough with a rolling pin.** Flatten the dough into a "pancake" and then roll it as if you were making a pastry piecrust. Roll it to the same $1/4$-inch or $1/2$-inch round as if you were shaping it by hand.

- **Allow the crust a short second rising of 20 minutes.** Transfer your rolled or patted-out dough to a baking sheet or baker's paddle that has been dusted with cornmeal. The cornmeal prevents the dough from sticking, but unlike flour, it doesn't leave a pasty taste. Another alternative is called a pizza screen; it's a flat, round pan with holes on it like a colander. The pizza screen is what I use because it makes it easier to transfer the pizza to and from the oven.

- **Preheat the oven.** Most pizzas are baked at 450°F, and it takes most ovens at least 15 minutes to reach that high a temperature. There are specific pizza stones on the market that are preheated on the bottom of the oven, and on which the pizza is baked. They replicate the hot, dry heat of a commercial oven. An alternative is to use a metal baking sheet in the same way.

- **Top and bake the pizza.** Here's where the individual recipes come into play. Follow the directions.

- **Cutting the pizza.** Don't spend money on one of those wheels to cut pizza unless you love gadgets. The best implement to cut a pizza is a sharp pair of scissors.

PIZZA IN THE EXPRESS LANE

The instructions given above are for active dry yeast, but there is an alternative on the market—if your supermarket carries it—that can significantly speed up the process of making a pizza dough.

Rapid-rise yeast, also called instant yeast depending on the brand, was introduced about twenty-five years ago. Instant yeast is more finely ground and thus absorbs moisture faster, rapidly converting starch and sugars to carbon dioxide, the tiny bubbles that make the dough expand and stretch. This type of yeast has been genetically engineered from different strains of yeast. Here are the differences when you use it:

- Use 25 percent less yeast than you would use active dry yeast. Because it's more finely ground, it measures differently.

- There's no need to proof the yeast. Mix it into the other dry ingredients, and then add water that is 120–130°F.

- Eliminate the first rising time. There is no need for the dough to double in bulk to create the structure when using instant yeast. Allow the dough to rest for 10 minutes, and then form it into a pizza or bread loaf, and allow it the proper time for rising then specified.

Basic Pizza Dough

Here's your basic crust, with some ways to personalize it at the end.

Yield: 1¼ pounds (enough for one 12-inch pizza) | **Active time:** 10 minutes | **Start to finish:** 1½ hours

> 1 tablespoon active dry yeast
> ¾ cup plus 2 tablespoons warm water, 100–110°F
> 1 teaspoon granulated sugar
> 2 ¾ cups all-purpose flour, plus additional for working dough
> 1 teaspoon salt
> 1 tablespoon olive oil

1. Combine yeast, water, and sugar in a small cup; stir well to dissolve yeast. Let stand 10 minutes, or until foamy.
2. Combine flour and salt in a mixing bowl or in a food processor fitted with the steel blade. Add in yeast mixture, and then knead dough until elastic. Use oil to coat a mixing bowl, and then allow dough to rise.
3. Punch down and shape dough into a crust, and allow it to rise for an additional 20 minutes, covered with a damp towel. Top and bake dough according to individual recipes.

Note: The dough can be made up to deflating it after rising 1 day in advance. Wrap the ball loosely in plastic wrap, and refrigerate. Allow dough to reach room temperature before rolling and topping.

Variations:
- Add 2 tablespoons chopped fresh herbs (such as basil or oregano) or 1 tablespoon dried herbs to the flour and salt mixture before yeast is added.
- Substitute whole wheat flour for the all-purpose flour.
- Use 2½ cups all-purpose flour and ⅓ cup finely ground yellow cornmeal in place of the 2 ¾ cups flour.

SUPERMARKET ALTERNATIVES

There's a middle step between spending large amounts of money to have a pizza delivered or buying them frozen at the supermarket and starting from scratch. Almost every supermarket now sells balls of refrigerated pizza dough.

This shortcut is a godsend for busy people. You can walk into the house and turn on the oven to preheat. By the time the oven is ready, the pizza is ready to go into it. Most bags of dough tell you if the dough needs rising or is ready to shape. Try to buy dough that comes from a local pizzeria; it is less likely to contain any chemicals or preservatives.

The other alternative, and one I don't suggest, is the pre-baked crust; the popular brand is Boboli. Various supermarkets also sell generic bread crusts. The reason why these are not a good alternative is that the dough is cooked and crisp before the ingredients in the topping. If you are using a pre-baked crust, the toppings should all be ones that require no further cooking, and the pizza should be baked at 450°F for 8–12 minutes, rather than for the time specified in the recipe.

THE CALZONE CONNECTION

Calzone (pronounced *cal-ZONE-eh*) is a pizza that's baked in the form of a turnover. While the word sounds exotic, it means "trouser leg" in Italian. Each of the pizza dough recipes in this chapter makes 4 calzone, and the dough should be rolled into a circle that's 1/4 inch thick because it will be doubled. While, like a pizza, calzone are hand-holdable, they are an excellent way to serve heavy fillings that might have a tendency to fall off a thin crust.

The filling for the calzone is placed over one half of the circle; leave a generous rim of at least 1 inch. Moisten the dough edges with water (you can use a pastry brush, or just your finger). Fold the uncovered portion over the filling, making sure the filling is completely covered. At this point you have a semicircle.

The last step is to firmly press the edge together, and then crimp the edge to seal it firmly together. Unlike with a piecrust there is no need to cut in steam vents, and calzone bake in the same amount of time as a pizza.

TERRIFIC TOPPINGS

There's no question about it: Certain pizza toppings can go on just as they are, but others really benefit from some cooking prior to being sprinkled on a crust. In fact, one of my tests of a good pizzeria is whether or not they treat ingredients with this care. If a pizza arrives with dried-out mushrooms, it shows me they were tossed on raw.

Here is a list of the pizza toppings used most often:

- **Toppings that need no pre-cooking:** Thinly sliced onion, scallions, or red onion; sliced garlic; green or red bell pepper and chile peppers; fresh spinach leaves or other leafy green vegetables; fresh or dried herbs; any sort of cooked protein like chicken, ham, pepperoni, or meatballs; thinly sliced steak.

- **Toppings to pre-cook if using a pre-baked crust:** Thinly sliced onion, scallions, or red onion; green or red bell peppers and chile peppers.

- **Toppings that need pre-cooking:** Any sort of raw meat, including bacon, chicken, ground beef, or sausage; eggplant, zucchini, yellow squash; mushrooms; artichokes.

"Cheater's" Pizza Dough

This dough is cheating because it's made with baking powder rather than yeast, so it needs no time to rise. While it doesn't have the yeasty flavor and aroma of a real pizza crust, it sure is fast!

Yield: 1¼ pounds (enough for one 12-inch pizza) | **Active time:** 15 minutes | **Start to finish:** 15 minutes

> 2 ¾ cups all-purpose flour, plus extra for rolling dough
> 1 teaspoon salt
> 1 teaspoon baking powder
> 4 tablespoons (½ stick) unsalted butter, cut into small bits and softened
> ¾ cup whole milk

1. Combine flour, salt, and baking powder in a mixing bowl. Cut in butter using a pastry blender, two knives, or your fingertips until mixture resembles coarse meal. This can also be done in a food processor fitted with the steel blade.
2. Add milk and stir until a soft dough forms. Place dough on a floured surface, and roll into a 12-inch circle. Top and bake as directed.

Note: The dough can be prepared for rolling up to 1 day in advance and refrigerated as a ball covered in plastic wrap.

> While baking powder is not alive the way yeast is, it doesn't last forever. If you haven't used it in some time, stir some into cool water. If it doesn't fizz a lot, you need a new can.

Basic Pizza Sauce

I'm a purist when it comes to the thick tomato sauce coating the crust of my pizzas; I like an intense tomato flavor and that's it. If you want flavors other than tomato, look at the variations listed beneath the recipe.

Yield: 2½ cups | **Active time:** 10 minutes | **Start to finish:** 30 minutes

> 2 tablespoons olive oil
> 1 small onion, peeled and finely chopped
> 2 garlic cloves, peeled and minced
> 1 (28-ounce) can crushed tomatoes in tomato puree
> Salt and freshly ground black pepper to taste

1. Heat oil in a large saucepan over medium-high heat. Add onion and garlic, and cook, stirring frequently, for 3 minutes, or until onion is translucent.
2. Add tomatoes, and bring to a boil. Reduce the heat to low, and simmer sauce, uncovered, for 20 minutes, or until reduced by ⅓, stirring occasionally. Season sauce to taste with salt and pepper.

Note: The sauce can be refrigerated for up to 5 days, and can be frozen for up to 6 months.

Variations:
- Add 1 tablespoon Italian seasoning to the sauce.
- Increase the garlic to 4 cloves.
- Add ½ cup dry red wine, and simmer the sauce for an additional 5 minutes.

> If you're freezing all or most of the sauce, it's best to freeze it in ½ cup portions. Most pizza recipes are written for either ½ or 1 cup sauce, so there will be no waste of sauce when using portions in the future.

Pizza Margherita

Queen Margherita was the wife of Italy's King Umberto I at the end of the nineteenth century. This simple pizza with red tomatoes and white mozzarella flecked with fresh green basil—the colors of the Italian flag—was created in her honor by a pizza maker in Naples.

Yield: 4–6 servings | **Active time:** 10 minutes | **Start to finish:** 40 minutes

> 1 recipe Basic Pizza Dough (recipe on page 176) or 1¼ pounds purchased pizza dough
> 6 ripe plum tomatoes, rinsed, cored, seeded, and chopped
> Salt and freshly ground black pepper to taste
> ½ pound whole-milk mozzarella cheese, thinly sliced
> ¼ cup chopped fresh basil
> 3 tablespoons olive oil

1. Preheat the oven to 450°F, and place a baking stone or baking sheet on the bottom of the oven. Form pizza dough into 1 large pizza or 4–6 individual rounds. Allow crusts to rise for 20 minutes, lightly covered with a damp towel.
2. Place tomatoes in a mixing bowl, and sprinkle them with salt and pepper. Allow tomatoes to sit for 15 minutes, then drain in a colander.
3. Arrange cheese on top of dough, and sprinkle tomatoes and basil on top. Drizzle with olive oil, and sprinkle with additional salt and pepper.
4. Bake pizza on pizza stone or baking sheet for 10 minutes. Reduce the oven temperature to 400°F, and bake for an additional 10–15 minutes, or until crust is golden. Serve immediately.

Note: The pizza can be prepared for baking up to 30 minutes in advance and kept at room temperature.

Variations:
- Substitute oregano for the basil.
- Stir 2 garlic cloves, peeled and minced, into the olive oil before drizzling it on the pizza.

Ratatouille Pizza

Many members of my Parents Panel said that one way to get kids to try—and maybe even like!—new foods is to put them on top of a pizza; the theory is that the form is fun so maybe they'll be adventurous. Feel free to substitute other vegetables for those listed here to accomplish this goal.

Yield: 4–6 servings | **Active time:** 25 minutes | **Start to finish:** 45 minutes

1 recipe Basic Pizza Dough (recipe on page 176) or 1¼ pounds purchased pizza dough
3 tablespoons olive oil
½ small red onion, peeled and thinly sliced
2 garlic cloves, peeled and minced
1 small Japanese eggplant, rinsed, trimmed, and thinly sliced
1 small zucchini, rinsed, trimmed, and thinly sliced
1 small yellow squash, rinsed, trimmed, and thinly sliced
Salt and freshly ground black pepper to taste
¾ cup Basic Pizza Sauce (recipe on page 180) or purchased sauce
2 tablespoons chopped fresh parsley
1 teaspoon dried thyme
1¼ cups grated Swiss cheese

Adult additions:

2–4 anchovy fillets, cut into 1-inch pieces
½ cup sliced oil-cured black olives

1. Preheat the oven to 450°F, and place a baking stone or baking sheet on the bottom of the oven. Form pizza dough into 1 large pizza or 4–6 individual rounds. Allow crusts to rise for 20 minutes, lightly covered with a damp towel.
2. Heat oil in a large skillet over medium-high heat. Add onion and garlic, and cook for 2 minutes. Add eggplant, zucchini, and yellow squash, and cook for 3–5 minutes, or until vegetables are crisp-tender. Season to taste with salt and pepper, and set aside.
3. Spread crust with pizza sauce, stopping 1 inch from the edge. Sprinkle sauce with parsley and thyme. Arrange vegetables on top of sauce, and sprinkle with cheese. Add anchovy fillets and olives to adult portions, if desired, before sprinkling with cheese.

4. Bake pizza on pizza stone or baking sheet for 10 minutes. Reduce the oven temperature to 400°F, and bake for an additional 10–15 minutes, or until crust is golden. Serve immediately.

Note: The pizza can be prepared for baking up to 30 minutes in advance and kept at room temperature.

Variation:
- Substitute ½ green bell pepper, seeds and ribs removed, and thinly sliced, for the zucchini or yellow squash.

> Slender Japanese eggplants need no salting or soaking before being cooked because they don't have an innate bitterness to remove.

Tuna Melt Pizza

The first time I heard about this I gasped, but it's become an addiction in my kitchen! I can see why kids love it.

Yield: 4–6 servings | **Active time:** 10 minutes | **Start to finish:** 40 minutes

> 1 recipe Basic Pizza Dough (recipe on page 176) or 1¼ pounds purchased pizza dough
> 3 ripe plum tomatoes, rinsed, cored, seeded, and chopped
> Salt and freshly ground black pepper to taste
> ½ cup mayonnaise
> 2 (5-ounce) cans light tuna packed in oil, drained and flaked
> ½ cup sweet pickle relish
> 1½ cups grated cheddar cheese

Adult addition:
> 3 scallions, white parts and 3 inches of green tops, rinsed, trimmed, and sliced

1. Preheat the oven to 450°F, and place a baking stone or baking sheet on the bottom of the oven. Form pizza dough into 1 large pizza or 4–6 individual rounds. Allow crusts to rise for 20 minutes, lightly covered with a damp towel.
2. Place tomatoes in a mixing bowl, and sprinkle them with salt and pepper. Allow tomatoes to sit for 15 minutes, then drain in a colander.
3. Spread crust with mayonnaise, stopping 1 inch from the edge. Sprinkle tomatoes, tuna, and pickle relish over mayonnaise, and then sprinkle cheese over all. Add scallions to adult portions, if desired, before adding cheese.
4. Bake pizza on pizza stone or baking sheet for 10 minutes. Reduce the oven temperature to 400°F, and bake for an additional 10–15 minutes, or until crust is golden. Serve immediately.

Note: The pizza can be prepared for baking up to 30 minutes in advance and kept at room temperature.

Variation:
- Add 2 hard-cooked eggs, peeled and thinly sliced, along with the other toppings.

It's important to take the time to salt and drain the tomatoes. Ripe tomatoes contain a lot of moisture, and they can create a soggy crust if not pre-treated.

Barbecued Chicken Pizza

Here's a great way to stretch leftover chicken into a whole meal, and you can sneak in some mushrooms and other veggies on it, too.

Yield: 4–6 servings | **Active time:** 15 minutes | **Start to finish:** 40 minutes

> 1 recipe Basic Pizza Dough (recipe on page 176) or 1¼ pounds purchased pizza dough
> 2 tablespoons olive oil
> 1 medium zucchini, rinsed, trimmed, and thinly sliced
> ¼ pound mushrooms, wiped with a damp paper towel, trimmed, and thinly sliced
> Salt and freshly ground black pepper to taste
> ¾ cup barbecue sauce (homemade or purchased)
> 2 cups diced cooked chicken
> 1½ cups grated smoked cheddar cheese

Adult addition:
> ½ small red onion, peeled and thinly sliced

1. Preheat the oven to 450°F, and place a baking stone or baking sheet on the bottom of the oven. Form pizza dough into 1 large pizza or 4–6 individual rounds. Allow crusts to rise for 20 minutes, lightly covered with a damp towel.
2. Heat oil in a large skillet over medium-high heat. Add zucchini and mushrooms, and cook for 3–5 minutes, or until vegetables are crisp-tender. Sprinkle vegetables with salt and pepper, and set aside.
3. Spread sauce over pizza crust, stopping 1 inch from the edge. Sprinkle chicken and vegetables on top of sauce, and then sprinkle cheese on top. Add red onion to adult portions of pizza, if desired, before adding cheese.
4. Bake pizza on pizza stone or baking sheet for 10 minutes. Reduce the oven temperature to 400°F, and bake for an additional 10–15 minutes, or until crust is golden. Serve immediately.

Note: The pizza can be prepared for baking up to 30 minutes in advance and kept at room temperature.

Variations:
- Substitute Monterey Jack for the smoked cheddar.
- Substitute 1 green bell pepper, seeds and ribs removed, and thinly sliced, for the zucchini.

If you want the kids to help you prepare food, mushrooms are a good way to start, as long as you have an egg slicer. The slicer is not too sharp, and it creates perfect even slices, too.

Mexican Chicken Pizza

Adding some seasoning to the Basic Pizza Sauce instantly produces one with Mexican flavors, and the addition of beans and corn to the toppings on this pizza make it a healthful meal.

Yield: 4-6 servings | **Active time:** 15 minutes | **Start to finish:** 40 minutes

- 1 recipe Basic Pizza Dough (recipe on page 176) or ¼ pounds purchased pizza dough
- 2 tablespoons olive oil
- ½ small red onion, peeled and chopped
- 2 garlic cloves, peeled and minced
- 1 tablespoon chili powder
- 1 teaspoon ground cumin
- ¾ cup Basic Pizza Sauce (recipe on page 180) or purchased sauce
- 2 tablespoons chopped fresh cilantro
- 1 cup shredded cooked chicken
- ½ cup canned black beans, drained and rinsed
- ½ cup fresh corn kernels or frozen corn kernels, thawed
- 1½ cups grated Monterey Jack cheese

Adult additions:

- 1-2 jalapeño or serrano chiles, seeds and ribs removed, and thinly sliced
- ½ cup sliced pimiento-stuffed green olives

1. Preheat the oven to 450°F, and place a baking stone or baking sheet on the bottom of the oven. Form pizza dough into 1 large pizza or 4-6 individual rounds. Allow crusts to rise for 20 minutes, lightly covered with a damp towel.

2. Heat oil in a small saucepan over medium-high heat. Add onion and garlic, and cook, stirring frequently, for 3 minutes, or until onion is translucent. Add chili powder and cumin, and cook for 1 minute, stirring constantly. Add pizza sauce and cilantro, and bring to a boil. Reduce the heat to low, and simmer sauce, uncovered, for 5 minutes.

3. Spread sauce on crust, stopping 1 inch from the edge. Sprinkle chicken, beans, and corn on top of sauce, and sprinkle cheese over all. Add chiles and olives to adult portions, if desired, before adding cheese.

4. Bake pizza on pizza stone or baking sheet for 10 minutes. Reduce the oven temperature to 400°F, and bake for an additional 10–15 minutes, or until crust is golden. Serve immediately.

Note: The pizza can be prepared for baking up to 30 minutes in advance and kept at room temperature.

Variations:
- Substitute jalapeño Jack for the Monterey Jack over adult portions of the pizza.
- Substitute baked ham or roast pork for the chicken.

> This variation of pizza sauce is also excellent for enchiladas or any Hispanic dish requiring a tomato sauce, so keep some handy in the freezer.

Buffalo Chicken Pizza

You can vary the spicing to suit your kids' preferences, but this pizza really does deliver the flavor of Buffalo chicken, and the spiciness is toned down by the cheese.

Yield: 4–6 servings | **Active time:** 20 minutes | **Start to finish:** 40 minutes

> 1 recipe Basic Pizza Dough (recipe on page 176) or 1¼ pounds purchased pizza dough
> ½ pound boneless, skinless chicken breast halves
> 2 tablespoons unsalted butter
> ¾ cup Basic Pizza Sauce (recipe on page 180) or purchased sauce
> 1 tablespoon Worcestershire sauce
> Hot red pepper sauce to taste
> Salt and freshly ground black pepper to taste
> 1¼ cups grated whole-milk mozzarella cheese or Monterey Jack cheese

Adult addition:
> ½ cup crumbled blue cheese

1. Preheat the oven to 450°F, and place a baking stone or baking sheet on the bottom of the oven. Form pizza dough into 1 large pizza or 4–6 individual rounds. Allow crusts to rise for 20 minutes, lightly covered with a damp towel.

2. Rinse chicken and pat dry with paper towels. Trim chicken of all visible fat, and cut into ½-inch slices against the grain.

3. Heat butter in a skillet over medium-high heat. Add chicken, and stir-fry for 1 minute, or until slices are opaque. Add pizza sauce, Worcestershire sauce, and hot red pepper sauce. Cook for 3–5 minutes, or until chicken is cooked through and no longer pink. Season to taste with salt and pepper.

4. Spread chicken and sauce on top of dough, and sprinkle with cheese. Sprinkle blue cheese over adult portions, if desired.

5. Bake pizza on pizza stone or baking sheet for 10 minutes. Reduce the oven temperature to 400°F, and bake for an additional 10–15 minutes, or until crust is golden. Serve immediately.

Note: The pizza can be prepared for baking up to 30 minutes in advance and kept at room temperature.

Mighty Meaty Pizza

Here's a pizza version of spaghetti with Bolognese sauce, and kids adore it. Serve it with a tossed salad, and your dinner is complete.

Yield: 4–6 servings | **Active time:** 20 minutes | **Start to finish:** 40 minutes

> 1 recipe Basic Pizza Dough (recipe on page 176) or 1¼ pounds purchased pizza dough
> 1 tablespoon olive oil
> ¼ pound ground chuck
> ¼ pound sweet or spicy bulk Italian sausage
> ¼ pound sliced pepperoni
> 1 cup Basic Pizza Sauce (recipe on page 180) or purchased sauce
> 1¼ cups grated whole-milk mozzarella cheese
> ¼ cup freshly grated Parmesan cheese

Adult addition:
> Crushed red pepper flakes to taste

1. Preheat the oven to 450°F, and place a baking stone or baking sheet on the bottom of the oven. Form pizza dough into 1 large pizza or 4–6 individual rounds. Allow crusts to rise for 20 minutes, lightly covered with a damp towel.
2. Heat oil in a large skillet over medium-high heat. Add ground chuck and sausage, and cook, breaking up lumps with a fork, for 3–5 minutes, or until browned and no pink remains. Remove meats from the skillet with a slotted spoon, and discard fat from the skillet.
3. Return meats to the skillet, and add pepperoni and sauce. Bring to a boil, reduce the heat to low, and simmer sauce, uncovered, for 5 minutes.
4. Spread mixture on crust, stopping 1 inch from the edge. Sprinkle mozzarella and Parmesan on top of meats. Sprinkle crushed red pepper flakes over adult portions, if desired.
5. Bake pizza on pizza stone or baking sheet for 10 minutes. Reduce the oven temperature to 400°F, and bake for an additional 10–15 minutes, or until crust is golden. Serve immediately.

Note: The pizza can be prepared for baking up to 30 minutes in advance and kept at room temperature.

Hawaiian Pizza

In all honesty, I don't understand the popularity of putting pineapple on a pizza for anyone of any age, but I've been told to include it because kids like it. It's also one of the most popular pizzas sold in Australia, so it has international appeal.

Yield: 4–6 servings | **Active time:** 10 minutes | **Start to finish:** 40 minutes

> 1 recipe Basic Pizza Dough (recipe on page 176) or 1¼ pounds purchased pizza dough
> 1 cup Basic Pizza Sauce (recipe on page 180) or purchased sauce
> 1 (6-ounce) can pineapple tidbits, well drained
> 1 cup diced cooked ham
> 1½ cups grated whole-milk mozzarella cheese or Monterey Jack cheese

1. Preheat the oven to 450°F, and place a baking stone or baking sheet on the bottom of the oven. Form pizza dough into 1 large pizza or 4–6 individual rounds. Allow crusts to rise for 20 minutes, lightly covered with a damp towel.
2. Spread sauce on top of crust, stopping 1 inch from the edge. Sprinkle pineapple and ham on top of sauce, and sprinkle cheese on top of the other ingredients.
3. Bake pizza on pizza stone or baking sheet for 10 minutes. Reduce the oven temperature to 400°F, and bake for an additional 10–15 minutes, or until crust is golden. Serve immediately.

Note: The pizza can be prepared for baking up to 30 minutes in advance and kept at room temperature.

Variations:
- Substitute Canadian bacon or cooked chicken for the ham.
- Substitute jalapeño Jack cheese for all or some of the mozzarella cheese on the adult portions.

> If you're using commercial sauce and not your own pizza sauce, make sure to use pizza sauce and not marinara or spaghetti sauce. These sauces are too thin to properly coat a pizza.

"Green Eggs and Ham" Pizza

Here is my homage to beloved Dr. Seuss. The eggs aren't green, but they sit on a bed of spinach, so that color is represented! Here's a dish you could serve at brunch for families, too.

Yield: 4–6 servings | **Active time:** 15 minutes | **Start to finish:** 40 minutes

> 1 recipe Basic Pizza Dough (recipe on page 176) or 1¼ pounds purchased pizza dough
> 2 tablespoons olive oil
> 1 (10-ounce) package frozen chopped spinach, thawed
> Salt and freshly ground black pepper to taste
> 1 cup grated whole-milk mozzarella cheese
> ½ pound thinly sliced baked ham
> 4–6 large eggs
> ¼ cup freshly grated Parmesan cheese

1. Preheat the oven to 450°F, and place a baking stone or baking sheet on the bottom of the oven. Form pizza dough into 1 large pizza or 4–6 individual rounds. Allow crusts to rise for 20 minutes, lightly covered with a damp towel.
2. Brush crust with oil. Place spinach in a colander, and press with the back of a spoon to extract as much liquid as possible. Scatter spinach evenly over crust, stopping 1 inch from the edge. Sprinkle spinach with salt and pepper, and sprinkle mozzarella cheese on top of spinach.
3. Create 4–6 "nests" with ham slices by rolling them into cups in your hand and then placing them on pizza. Break 1 egg into each. Sprinkle eggs with salt and pepper, and sprinkle with Parmesan cheese.
4. Bake pizza on pizza stone or baking sheet for 10 minutes. Reduce the oven temperature to 400°F, and bake for an additional 10–15 minutes, or until crust is golden. Serve immediately.

Note: The pizza can be prepared for baking up to 30 minutes in advance and kept at room temperature.

Variations:
- Substitute chopped broccoli for the spinach.
- Substitute smoked turkey for the ham.
- Substitute cheddar cheese for the mozzarella.

Bacon, Tomato, and Cheddar Pizza

A grilled cheese sandwich with bacon and tomato is my way of pampering myself with comfort food. These ingredients also make good toppings for a pizza. Serve this with a tossed salad.

Yield: 4–6 servings | **Active time:** 20 minutes | **Start to finish:** 40 minutes

> 1 recipe Basic Pizza Dough (recipe on page 176) or 1¼ pounds purchased pizza dough
> 4 ripe plum tomatoes, rinsed, cored, seeded, and chopped
> Salt and freshly ground black pepper to taste
> ½ pound bacon, cut into 1-inch lengths
> 1½ cups grated sharp cheddar cheese

Adult addition:
> 2–3 tablespoons Dijon mustard

1. Preheat the oven to 450°F, and place a baking stone or baking sheet on the bottom of the oven. Form pizza dough into 1 large pizza or 4–6 individual rounds. Allow crusts to rise for 20 minutes, lightly covered with a damp towel.
2. Place tomatoes in a mixing bowl, and sprinkle them with salt and pepper. Allow tomatoes to sit for 15 minutes, then drain in a colander.
3. While tomatoes sit, place bacon in a skillet over medium-high heat. Cook for 5–7 minutes, or until brown and crisp. Remove bacon from the pan with a slotted spoon, and drain on paper towels.
4. Spread mustard over dough on adult portions, if desired. Arrange cheese on top of dough, and sprinkle tomatoes and bacon on top.
5. Bake pizza on pizza stone or baking sheet for 10 minutes. Reduce the oven temperature to 400°F, and bake for an additional 10–15 minutes, or until crust is golden. Serve immediately.

Note: The pizza can be prepared for baking up to 30 minutes in advance and kept at room temperature.

Variations:
- Substitute Swiss cheese for the cheddar cheese.
- Substitute Canadian bacon, sliced smoked turkey, or sliced baked ham for the bacon; these foods need no additional cooking.

Chapter 9:
Dishes with Asian Accents

Adding more vegetables to your kids' diets is a benefit of serving Asian food. And eating the bits of crunchy vegetables with chopsticks makes for mealtime fun too. There are lots of finger foods in Asian cooking, as well as dishes threaded onto bamboo skewers; these are always a hit with kids.

While fiery Szechwan and Thai foods have become more popular in recent decades, the basis for most of the recipes in this chapter is mildly seasoned Cantonese-inspired cooking, and some dishes contain fruits as well as vegetables. I've also given many hints on spicing up these quick stir-fries for you, too.

Asian recipes, like the menu in a Chinese restaurant, are built around substitutions. So if you find your kids like a particular sauce, there are myriad ways that you can use it again, and introduce them to different foods.

BECOMING A CHAMP WITH CHOPSTICKS

Using chopsticks for eating Asian food turns an ordinary family meal into a fun game for the kids. More than one picky eater has been known to eat many an Occidental dish with chopsticks, too.

To learn to use chopsticks, it helps if you think of them as a pair of tongs and your hand serves as the hinge with one stick held firmly and the other one moved up and down. There is no one definitive way to hold the chopsticks. As long as you can comfortably pick up the food and bring it to your mouth, you are using the chopsticks correctly.

Pick up the first chopstick with the middle finger and thumb. Stiffen your hand for a firm grip. Lay the broad end of the chopstick on the part where your thumb and index finger connect. Rest the narrow end on the tip of your ring finger, and hold it in place with the tip of your middle finger. This part is constant, but there are a few alternatives for making them work.

The first method is to grip the second chopstick with your index finger. Place your thumb over the second chopstick. Adjust your grip to a more comfortable position. Make sure the narrow tips of the chopsticks are even with each other to help prevent them from crossing or being unable to "pinch" the food. Hold it steady. This chopstick should not move when you attempt to pick up food.

Alternatively, hold the first chopstick steady and move the second (top) chopstick by moving the tip of your index finger up and down while the thumb remains relatively steady, acting like a pivot point. The top chopstick remains pressed to the index finger from the tip through the first joint. The movement comes from flexing the joint closest to the knuckle. Straightening your index finger opens the chopsticks and bending it closes them, with perhaps a slight flexing of the thumb to keep the chopsticks lined up with each other.

Practice opening and closing the chopsticks. Make sure the broad ends of the chopsticks do not make an X as this will make it difficult to pick up food. Pick up food at a good angle (try roughly 45 degrees from the plate); lift it up a few inches. If it feels unstable, put it down and try again. Apply a firm but gentle pressure on the food, just enough to keep the food from falling from the chopsticks. Too much pressure is more likely to cause your chopsticks to cross at the narrow ends unless they're perfectly aligned, and could launch your food across the table.

If you watch Asian people eating, it helps to master this process, but start by using "training wheels." Asians will hold their chopsticks very far up toward the thick ends, but they are easier to control if you hold them closer to the thin ends. And practice is the key to success, so if you're really interested in learning, use chopsticks at home when eating any food with small bits, like a stew, too.

SUCCESSFUL STIR-FRYING

For stir-frying, advance planning, speed, and control are the keys to success. The ancient Chinese invented stir-frying as one of their more than 50 methods of food preparation. However, many recipes now utilize the technique for non-Asian dishes. It's quick, requires little fat, and leaves food with the crisp-tender texture we enjoy today.

Because the final cooking is a quick process, the food must be sitting in bowls or dishes placed within arm's reach, ready to be cooked. Cut all pieces of the same ingredient the same size, have your seasonings at hand, and make sure that any required partial cooking of vegetables—such as blanching green beans—has already been done.

The game plan is that when the dish comes to the table all the ingredients are properly cooked, so there are two options: Either cut food that takes longer to cook into smaller pieces and cook everything at the same time, or start with the longer-cooking food and keep adding ingredients in their decreasing need of time. Both strategies produce good results. Never place too much food in the wok or skillet at one time. The food must be able to be seared on all sides, without steaming from being buried under a layer of food.

While it's possible to adapt many recipes to stir-frying, oil rather than butter should be used. The dairy solids in butter burn at a very low temperature, 250°F, so it can only be added as a flavoring agent once food is cooked. Oil, on the other hand, does not begin to smoke until it is heated to more than 400°F, so it is the better choice. There is no consensus as to what oil to use; that's why I lump them together as vegetable oil in the ingredient lists. Peanut, corn, soy, or canola all work well. Olive oil will give the dish a pronounced flavor, and it smokes at too low a temperature to be effective in sealing the food.

Place the wok or skillet over a high flame, and heat it very hot. Listen for the sound of sizzles; if a few drops of water evaporate immediately the pan is ready. Add the required amount of oil to the pan, and swirl it around gently to coat all sides.

Add the food, and keep it moving in the pan. If stir-frying in a wok, use a wire mesh spoon designed for the job. If stir-frying in a skillet, use a spoon that will reach to all places on the bottom, and with which you can keep food moving. In some recipes, liquid is added and the pan is covered for a brief time. In other recipes, it's fry and eat.

Curried Tofu with Dried Fruit

This recipe is a hybrid of Asian and Caribbean cuisines, which are united by their use of curry powder. Some chopped dried apricots add a sweet nuance, and healthful vegetables complement the tofu for nutritional value. Serve it over rice or egg noodles.

Yield: 4-6 servings | **Active time:** 15 minutes | **Start to finish:** 30 minutes

1 (14–16-ounce) package firm tofu
3 tablespoons vegetable oil
6 scallions, white parts and 4 inches of green tops, rinsed, trimmed, and sliced, divided
2 garlic cloves, peeled and minced
2 tablespoons grated fresh ginger
1–2 tablespoons curry powder, or to taste
1 (14-ounce) can light coconut milk
¼ cup soy sauce
2 large carrots, peeled and thinly sliced on the diagonal
2 celery ribs, rinsed, trimmed, and thinly sliced on the diagonal
1 cup shredded green cabbage
½ cup chopped dried apricots
1 tablespoon cornstarch
2 tablespoons cold water
Salt and freshly ground black pepper to taste
2–3 cups cooked rice, hot

1. Drain tofu, and cut into ¾-inch cubes. Set aside.
2. Heat oil in a wok or large skillet over high heat, swirling to coat the pan. Add ⅔ of scallions, garlic, and ginger to the pan, and stir-fry for 30 seconds, or until fragrant. Stir in curry powder, and cook for 30 seconds.
3. Stir coconut milk and soy sauce into the skillet, and bring to a boil, stirring frequently. Add tofu, carrots, celery, cabbage, and dried apricots. Bring to a boil, reduce the heat to medium-low, and simmer mixture, stirring occasionally, for 5–7 minutes, or until vegetables are crisp-tender.

4. Mix cornstarch and water in a small cup, and stir mixture into the pan. Cook for 2 minutes, or until slightly thickened. Season to taste with salt and pepper, and serve immediately, sprinkled with remaining scallions.

Note: The dish can be prepared for cooking up to 6 hours in advance and refrigerated, tightly covered.

Variation:
- Substitute 1 pound boneless, skinless chicken breast, cut into $^3/_4$-inch cubes for the tofu. Add chicken back into the pan along with vegetables, and cook until chicken is cooked through and no longer pink.

> While it's a good idea to toss out any dried herb or spice that's been opened for more than 6 months, abbreviate the life of curry powder to 2 months. This ground blend, made up of up to 20 herbs and spices, loses its flavor and aroma very quickly.

Stir-Fried Tofu with Green Beans

Many members of my Parents Panel swear by tofu as a sure-fire way to get some protein into their kids without a fight. For this dish, all the ingredients can be culled from the supermarket, too.

Yield: 4–6 servings | **Active time:** 25 minutes | **Start to finish:** 25 minutes

1 (14–16-ounce) package firm tofu
1/3 cup soy sauce, divided
2 tablespoons honey, divided
2 garlic cloves, peeled and minced, divided
3/4 cup Vegetable Stock (recipe on page 57) or purchased stock
1 tablespoon cornstarch
1 tablespoon cold water
3 tablespoons vegetable oil
3 scallions, white parts and 4 inches of green tops, rinsed, trimmed, and thinly sliced
2 tablespoons grated fresh ginger
1/2 pound fresh green beans, rinsed, trimmed, and cut into 1-inch pieces on the diagonal
Salt and freshly ground black pepper to taste

Adult addition:
1/2 teaspoon crushed red pepper flakes, or to taste

1. Drain tofu, and cut into 3/4-inch cubes. Combine 2 tablespoons soy sauce, 1 tablespoon honey, and 1 garlic clove in a mixing bowl. Stir well, add tofu, and set aside.

2. Combine remaining soy sauce, honey, and stock in a small bowl, and set aside. Combine cornstarch with water in a small bowl, stir well, and set aside.

3. Heat vegetable oil in a heavy wok or skillet over high heat, swirling to coat the pan. Add scallions, remaining garlic, and ginger, and stir-fry for 30 seconds, or until fragrant. Add tofu and green beans, and stir-fry for 2 minutes, stirring constantly.

4. Add sauce mixture and cook, stirring constantly, for 2 minutes, or until green beans are crisp-tender. Add cornstarch mixture and simmer for 1 minute, or until slightly thickened. Season to taste with salt and pepper, and serve immediately. Add crushed red pepper flakes to adult portions, if desired.

Note: The dish can be prepared up to cooking 6 hours in advance. Refrigerate chicken separately from vegetables.

Variation:
- Substitute broccoli, cut into florets, or asparagus, woody stems discarded and cut into 1-inch pieces on the diagonal, for the green beans.

Here's a way to minimize the number of bowls you'll have to wash after cooking a stir-fried dish: Layer the vegetables starting with the one added last at the bottom of the bowl, and separate the layers with plastic wrap. When it's time to add the next ingredient, just reach in, grab the sheet of plastic wrap, and toss in the ingredients.

Chicken in Lettuce Cups

This dish, served in healthful, crunchy lettuce cups, is like a Chinese version of a taco. The kids can roll it themselves, too, which adds to their participation in the meal.

Yield: 4–6 servings | **Active time:** 20 minutes | **Start to finish:** 20 minutes

2 tablespoons Asian sesame oil*
2 garlic cloves, peeled and minced
1 tablespoon grated fresh ginger
4 scallions, white parts and 3 inches of green tops, rinsed, trimmed, and thinly sliced
1 pound ground chicken
1 (8-ounce) can water chestnuts, drained, rinsed, and chopped
¼ cup soy sauce
2 tablespoons hoisin sauce*
1 tablespoon cider vinegar
2 teaspoons cornstarch
Salt and freshly ground black pepper to taste
36 (4-inch) rounds iceberg lettuce, rinsed and dried
½ cup chopped scallions (optional)

Adult addition:
1–2 teaspoons Chinese chili paste with garlic*

1. Heat sesame oil in a large skillet over medium-high heat. Add garlic, ginger, and scallions, and cook for 30 seconds, stirring constantly. Add chicken, breaking up lumps with a fork, and cook for 4–5 minutes or until chicken has lost all of its pink color and is white and beginning to brown. Stir in water chestnuts, and stir-fry 1 minute.

2. Mix soy sauce, hoisin sauce, vinegar, and cornstarch in a small bowl. Add to the pan, and when mixture boils and thickens, reduce the heat to low, and simmer for 1 minute, stirring frequently. Season to taste with salt and pepper. Add chili paste to adult portions, if desired.

3. Spoon mixture into lettuce leaves, and garnish with scallions, if using. Serve immediately.

*Available in the Asian aisle of most supermarkets and in specialty markets.

Note: The filling can be prepared up to 2 days in advance and refrigerated, tightly covered. Reheat it over low heat, covered, until hot, stirring occasionally.

Variation:

- Substitute ground pork or ground turkey for the ground chicken.

Hoisin sauce, pronounced *hoy-ZAHN,* is a thick sweet and spicy reddish brown sauce; it's made from a mixture of soybeans, garlic, chiles, Chinese five-spice powder, and sugar. Like ketchup in our country, it's used both as a condiment and as an ingredient.

Chicken Yakitori

Mildly seasoned yakitori is a traditional Japanese way of preparing skewered food. In this recipe some crunchy water chestnuts and bright green scallions join the tender morsels of chicken. Serve these with some rice and a steamed green vegetable.

Yield: 4–6 servings | **Active time:** 15 minutes | **Start to finish:** 2½ hours, including 2 hours for marinating

 1¼ pounds boneless, skinless chicken thighs
 ½ cup Japanese-style soy sauce
 ⅓ cup sake or dry sherry
 2 tablespoons granulated sugar
 1 tablespoon grated fresh ginger
 1 garlic clove, peeled and minced
 Freshly ground black pepper to taste
 8–10 scallions, white parts and 4 inches of green tops, cut into 1½-inch pieces
 1 (8-ounce) can whole water chestnuts, drained and rinsed
 12 (8-inch) bamboo skewers
 2–3 cups cooked rice, hot

1. Rinse chicken and pat dry with paper towels. Cut chicken into 1½-inch cubes. Combine soy sauce, sake or sherry, sugar, ginger, garlic, and pepper in a jar with a tight-fitting lid, and shake well.
2. Divide chicken, scallions, and water chestnuts onto skewers; be careful with water chestnuts so they do not split apart. Arrange skewers in a shallow dish, and pour marinade over skewers. Marinate, refrigerated, for 2 hours, turning skewers occasionally.
3. Light a gas or charcoal grill, or preheat the oven broiler. Remove skewers from marinade, and discard marinade. Grill or broil skewers for a total of 10–15 minutes, turning them with tongs, or until chicken is cooked through and no longer pink. Serve immediately.

Note: The chicken can be marinated for up to 8 hours. The skewers can also be cooked 1 day in advance, and refrigerated, tightly covered. Serve them cold.

Variation:
 • Substitute boneless pork loin for the chicken.

Teriyaki Pork Chops

The sweet flavors that are part of traditional Japanese teriyaki preparations make these dishes very popular with kids. Some fried rice and a stir-fried vegetable would complete your meal.

Yield: 4–6 servings | **Active time:** 15 minutes | **Start to finish:** 3½ hours, including 3 hours for marinating

1½ pounds boneless pork loin
½ cup Japanese-style soy sauce
¼ cup mirin* or cream sherry
¼ cup rice wine vinegar*
¼ cup firmly packed light brown sugar
2 tablespoons grated fresh ginger
2 garlic cloves, peeled and minced
Freshly ground black pepper to taste

1. Rinse pork and pat dry with paper towels. Cut pork into 4–6 portions.
2. Combine soy sauce, mirin or sherry, vinegar, brown sugar, ginger, garlic, and pepper in a heavy resealable plastic bag. Mix well to dissolve sugar, and add pork. Marinate for 3 hours, refrigerated, turning the bag occasionally.
3. Light a charcoal or gas grill, or preheat the oven broiler. Remove pork from marinade, and transfer marinade to a small saucepan. Bring marinade to a boil, then reduce the heat to low, and simmer marinade for 5 minutes. Set aside.
4. Grill or broil pork for 4–5 minutes per side, or to desired doneness. Serve immediately, drizzled with marinade.

Note: The pork can marinate for up to 8 hours.

Variation:
- Substitute boneless, skinless chicken thighs for the pork. Bake chicken in a 425°F oven for 20–25 minutes, or until it registers 165°F with an instant-read thermometer.

*Available in the Asian aisle of most supermarkets and in specialty markets.

Mock Mu Shu Chicken

Easy to find and inexpensive flour tortillas are substitutes for Mandarin pancakes in this healthful stir-fried dish; let the kids smear the plum sauce on the tortillas and roll them up themselves. Serve it with some fried rice.

Yield: 4–6 servings | **Active time:** 25 minutes | **Start to finish:** 25 minutes

6 large dried shiitake mushrooms*
1 ounce dried wood ear mushrooms*
1 cup boiling water
³/₄ pound boneless, skinless chicken breast halves
¹/₄ cup soy sauce
1 tablespoon dry sherry
2 tablespoons cornstarch
2 tablespoons vegetable oil
4 scallions, white parts and 4 inches of green tops, rinsed, trimmed, and sliced
3 garlic cloves, peeled and minced
1¹/₂ cups shredded green cabbage
3 large eggs, lightly beaten
Salt and freshly ground black pepper to taste
¹/₂ cup plum sauce*
12 (6-inch) flour or whole-wheat tortillas

1. Place dried shiitake mushrooms and wood ear mushrooms into a small mixing bowl. Pour boiling water over mushrooms, pressing them into water with the back of a spoon. Soak mushrooms for 10 minutes, then drain, squeezing out as much liquid as possible. Discard stems, and slice mushrooms thinly. Set aside.
2. Rinse chicken and pat dry with paper towels. Trim chicken of all visible fat. Cut chicken into thin slivers by cutting into thin slices and then cutting slices lengthwise. Combine soy sauce, sherry, and cornstarch in a mixing bowl. Stir well, and add chicken to mixing bowl. Toss to coat chicken evenly.

*Available in the Asian aisle of most supermarkets and in specialty markets.

3. Heat oil in a wok or large skillet over medium-high heat. Add scallions and garlic and stir-fry for 30 seconds, or until fragrant. Add cabbage and chicken and stir-fry for 2 minutes, or until chicken is cooked through and no longer pink. Add mushrooms and eggs to the skillet, and stir. Cook for 1 minute, then scrape the bottom of the pan to dislodge cooked egg. Cook for an additional 1–2 minutes, or until eggs are just set. Season to taste with salt and pepper.

4. To serve, spread plum sauce on the surface of each tortilla. Place a portion of filling in the center. Tuck one edge over filling, and roll tortillas firmly to enclose filling. Serve immediately.

Note: The dish can be prepared up to cooking 6 hours in advance. Refrigerate chicken separately from vegetables.

Variation:
- Substitute boneless pork loin for the chicken.

Wood ear mushrooms, also called cloud ear, are a form of Asian dried mushroom with a slightly crunchy texture and very delicate flavor. They are almost brownish black and expand to five times their size when rehydrated.

Sweet-and-Sour Pork

Most Americans were introduced to Chinese-American food as kids with some sort of sweet-and-sour dish, and they appeal to all generations. This has lots of vegetables in it, so some rice is all you need to add.

Yield: 4–6 servings | **Active time:** 25 minutes | **Start to finish:** 25 minutes

- 1 pound boneless pork loin
- ³/₄ cup pineapple juice
- ¹/₂ cup ketchup
- ¹/₃ cup firmly packed light brown sugar
- ¹/₄ cup cider vinegar
- ¹/₄ cup water
- 2 tablespoons soy sauce
- 1 tablespoon cornstarch
- 2 tablespoons Asian sesame oil*
- 1 tablespoon vegetable oil
- 3 scallions, white parts and 4 inches of green tops, rinsed, trimmed, and chopped
- 2 garlic cloves, peeled and minced
- 2 tablespoons grated fresh ginger
- 1 sweet onion, such as Vidalia or Bermuda, peeled, and sliced lengthwise
- 1 green bell pepper, seeds and ribs removed, and sliced
- 2 cups diced fresh pineapple
- 2–3 cups cooked rice, hot

Adult addition:
- ¹/₂ teaspoon crushed red pepper flakes, or to taste

1. Rinse pork and pat dry with paper towels. Trim pork of all visible fat, and cut it into ³/₄-inch cubes. Set aside. Combine pineapple juice, ketchup, brown sugar, vinegar, water, soy sauce, and cornstarch in a bowl, and stir well to dissolve sugar. Set aside.
2. Heat sesame oil and vegetable oil in a wok or large skillet over high heat, swirling to coat the pan. Add pork, scallions, garlic, and ginger, and stir-fry for 2 minutes. Add onion and bell pepper and stir-fry for

*Available in the Asian aisle of most supermarkets and in specialty markets.

3 minutes, or until pork is cooked through. Add sauce and pineapple, and cook, stirring frequently, for 2 minutes, or until slightly thickened. Add crushed red pepper flakes to adult portions, if desired. Serve immediately.

Note: The dish can be cooked up to 1 day in advance and refrigerated, tightly covered. Reheat it in a 350°F oven, covered, for 15–20 minutes, or until hot.

Variations:
- Substitute boneless, skinless chicken breast for the pork.
- Substitute mango or papaya for the pineapple.

When cornstarch is added to a liquid mixture, it becomes cloudy. The way to know the sauce is done is both when it thickens and when it becomes clear again.

Pork Lo Mein

While Cantonese lo mein is traditionally made with long egg noodles, spaghetti works just fine, and kids like this dish because they are familiar with the pasta. This is not spicy, but the dish has lots of flavor, as well as a large amount of healthful and inexpensive cabbage.

Yield: 4–6 servings | **Active time:** 15 minutes | **Start to finish:** 30 minutes

½ pound spaghetti, broken into 2-inch lengths
8 large dried shiitake mushrooms*
½ cup boiling water
1 pound boneless pork loin
1 tablespoon cornstarch
4 tablespoons soy sauce, divided
Freshly ground black pepper to taste
3 tablespoons Asian sesame oil*
12 scallions, white parts and 4 inches of green tops, rinsed, trimmed, and sliced, divided
4 garlic cloves, peeled and minced
2 tablespoons grated fresh ginger
2 celery ribs, rinsed, trimmed, and sliced
2 cups shredded green cabbage
1 carrot, peeled and thinly sliced
⅓ cup oyster sauce*
½ cup Chicken Stock (recipe on page 55) or purchased stock

1. Bring a large pot of salted water to a boil. Add spaghetti, and cook according to package directions until al dente. Drain, and set aside. Pour boiling water over dried mushrooms, and push mushrooms down into liquid with the back of a spoon. Allow mushrooms to soak for 10 minutes, then drain, reserving soaking water. Discard mushroom stems, and slice thinly. Strain soaking water through paper coffee filter or paper towel, and set aside.
2. Rinse pork and pat dry with paper towels. Trim pork of all visible fat. Cut pork into ½-inch slices, then stack slices and cut into ½-inch-thick ribbons. Stir cornstarch into 2 tablespoons soy sauce, and stir mixture into pork. Season pork to taste with pepper, and set aside.

*Available in the Asian aisle of most supermarkets and in specialty markets.

3. Heat sesame oil in a wok or large skillet over medium-high heat. Add ⅓ of scallions, garlic, and ginger. Cook, stirring constantly, for 30 seconds, or until fragrant. Add pork to the pan, and cook, stirring constantly, for 2–3 minutes, or until pork is brown on both sides. Remove pork from the pan with a slotted spoon, and set aside.

4. Add remaining scallions, celery, cabbage, and carrot to the pan. Cook, stirring constantly, for 2 minutes. Add reserved mushrooms, mushroom soaking liquid, oyster sauce, stock, and remaining soy sauce to pan. Cover and cook 5 minutes, or until vegetables are crisp-tender. Uncover the pan, stir in pasta and pork, and cook an additional 2–3 minutes, or until pasta is hot. Serve immediately.

Note: The dish can be prepped up to 6 hours in advance and refrigerated, tightly covered.

Variations:

- Substitute boneless, skinless chicken thighs, cut into ½-inch dice, for the pork. Do not remove chicken from the pan before cooking vegetables so that chicken will be cooked through and no longer pink.
- Substitute sirloin tips for the pork loin, cut into thin strips, and substitute Beef Stock (recipe on page 56) for Chicken Stock. Cook beef for 1–2 minutes, or until browned.
- Substitute ¾ pound mushrooms, wiped with a damp paper towel, trimmed, and sliced, for the pork, and substitute Vegetable Stock (recipe on page 57) for Chicken Stock. Cook mushrooms along with other vegetables.

Stir-Fried Beef with Broccoli and Oranges

Sweet oranges, colorful broccoli, and traditional Asian seasonings are joined in this dish. All you need to complete the meal is some rice; the vegetables are already there.

Yield: 4–6 servings | **Active time:** 20 minutes | **Start to finish:** 20 minutes

> 2 navel oranges, rinsed in warm soapy water
> 3 tablespoons soy sauce
> 1 pound sirloin tips
> 3 tablespoons Asian sesame oil*
> 6 scallions, white parts and 4 inches of green tops, rinsed, trimmed, and chopped, divided
> 2 garlic cloves, peeled and minced
> 1 tablespoon grated fresh ginger
> 2 cups broccoli florets
> 1 tablespoon cornstarch
> 2 tablespoons cold water
> 2–3 cups cooked rice, hot

Adult addition:
> ½–1 teaspoon Chinese chile oil*

1. Grate zest of 1 orange into a mixing bowl, and squeeze juice from orange. Add soy sauce to the mixing bowl, and set aside. Peel and cut white pith from the other orange, and dice flesh into ¾-inch cubes. Set aside. Cut beef into ½-inch-thick slices. Set aside.
2. Heat oil in a wok or large, heavy skillet over high heat, swirling to coat the pan. Add beef, and stir-fry for 1–2 minutes, or until beef is no longer pink. Remove beef from the pan with a slotted spoon, and set aside.
3. Add ⅔ of scallions, garlic, and ginger to the pan, and stir-fry for 30 seconds, or until fragrant. Add broccoli, and stir-fry for 2 minutes. Return beef to the pan and add orange and orange juice mixture. Cook for 3 minutes, or until broccoli is crisp-tender.
4. Mix cornstarch with water in a small cup. Add to the pan, and cook for 1 minute, or until slightly thickened. Stir in remaining scallions, and serve immediately. Add chile oil to adult portions, if desired.

*Available in the Asian aisle of most supermarkets and in specialty markets.

Note: The dish can be prepared for cooking up to 6 hours in advance and refrigerated.

Variation:
- Substitute boneless pork loin for the beef.

Citrus fruits are often coated with wax before being shipped to help them keep longer. If using the zest of a citrus fruit, such as in this recipe, it's always a good idea to wash it with soapy water to remove the wax coating.

Stir-Fried Beef in Lettuce Cups

Here's a Korean take on the "lettuce taco," and it also includes some ginger and a bit of brown sugar that your kids will like. You can also serve it over rice or turn it into a lo mein by mixing it with spaghetti.

Yield: 4–6 servings | **Active time:** 20 minutes | **Start to finish:** 20 minutes

- 1 pound sirloin tips
- ¼ cup soy sauce
- 2 tablespoons Asian sesame oil*
- 2 tablespoons firmly packed dark brown sugar
- 2 garlic cloves, peeled and minced
- 1 tablespoon grated fresh ginger
- 1 tablespoon cornstarch
- 3 tablespoons vegetable oil, divided
- 1 medium sweet onion, such as Vidalia or Bermuda, peeled, halved, and cut into ½-inch slices
- 1 green bell pepper, seeds and ribs removed, and cut into ½-inch strips
- 12–18 iceberg lettuce leaves
- 2 scallions, white parts and 4 inches of green tops, rinsed, trimmed, and thinly sliced (optional)

Adult addition:
- ½–1 teaspoon Chinese chile oil*

1. Rinse beef and pat dry with paper towels. Cut beef into ½-inch slices against the grain. Place beef in a mixing bowl. Combine soy sauce, sesame oil, brown sugar, garlic, and ginger in a small bowl, and stir well. Toss beef with ½ of mixture and cornstarch.

2. Heat 1 tablespoon oil in a wok or large skillet over high heat, swirling to coat the pan. Add onion and green bell pepper, and stir-fry for 3 minutes. Remove vegetables from the pan with a slotted spoon, and set aside.

3. Heat remaining oil in the pan, swirling to coat the pan. Add beef, and stir-fry for 1–2 minutes, or until no pink remains. Return vegetables to the pan, and add remaining sauce mixture. Cook for 1 minute, or until slightly thickened.

*Available in the Asian aisle of most supermarkets and in specialty markets.

4. Add chile oil to adult portions, if desired. Spoon mixture into lettuce leaves, and garnish with scallions, if using. Serve immediately.

Note: The dish can be prepared for cooking up to 6 hours in advance, and refrigerated, tightly covered.

Variation:
- Substitute boneless pork loin for the beef.

The use of brown sugar in cooking is one of the hallmarks of Korean cuisine, which draws other culinary influences from both China and Japan.

Singapore-Style Curried Beef and Noodles

The foods of Singapore reflect its geographic location, close to Thailand, Malaysia, and China. The curry in this dish is very subtle, and is tamed with coconut milk.

Yield: 4–6 servings | **Active time:** 25 minutes | **Start to finish:** 25 minutes

½ pound spaghetti
3 tablespoons vegetable oil, divided
½ cup Beef Stock (recipe on page 56) or purchased stock
2 tablespoons dry sherry
2 tablespoons soy sauce
2 tablespoons coconut milk
1 tablespoon molasses
1 tablespoon curry powder
1 tablespoon cornstarch
3 scallions, white parts and 4 inches of green tops, rinsed, trimmed, and chopped
2 tablespoons grated fresh ginger
1 garlic clove, peeled and minced
½ pound ground chuck
2 cups firmly packed shredded green cabbage
1 green bell pepper, seeds and ribs removed, and very thinly sliced

Adult addition:
1–2 teaspoons Chinese chile oil*

1. Bring a large pot of salted water to a boil, and cook spaghetti according to package instructions until al dente. Drain, return spaghetti to the pot to keep warm, and toss with 1 tablespoon oil.
2. Combine stock, sherry, soy sauce, coconut milk, molasses, curry powder, and cornstarch in a small bowl, and stir well.
3. Heat remaining oil in a wok or large skillet over high heat, swirling to coat the pan. Add scallions, ginger, and garlic, and stir-fry for 30 seconds, or until fragrant. Add beef, breaking up lumps with a fork, and cook for 3 minutes, or until browned. Add cabbage and green bell pepper, and cook for an additional 2 minutes. Add sauce mixture, and cook for 2–3 minutes, or until slightly thickened.

*Available in the Asian aisle of most supermarkets and in specialty markets.

4. Add sauce to pasta, and cook over medium-high heat for 1–2 minutes, or until pasta is hot. Add chile oil to adult portions, if desired. Serve immediately.

Note: The dish can be prepared for cooking up to 6 hours in advance and refrigerated, tightly covered.

Variation:
- Substitute ground turkey or ground pork for the ground beef, and substitute Chicken Stock (recipe on page 55) for Beef Stock.

> Coconut milk should always be stirred well before being measured and added to a dish because, depending on the brand, there can be a hard layer of solids that rises to the top.

Sukiyaki

If you have an electric skillet, you can cook this at the table; it's the way they make it in Japan and in Japanese restaurants. The flavors are subtle, and there are lots of veggies! Serve it over rice.

Yield: 4–6 servings | **Active time:** 20 minutes | **Start to finish:** 20 minutes

1 pound sirloin tips
1 cup Beef Stock (recipe on page 56) or purchased stock
$\frac{1}{2}$ cup Japanese-style soy sauce
$\frac{1}{4}$ cup mirin* or cream sherry
3 tablespoons granulated sugar
2 tablespoons vegetable oil
2 medium onions, peeled, halved lengthwise, and thinly sliced
$\frac{1}{4}$ pound mushrooms, wiped with a damp paper towel, trimmed, and sliced
2 celery ribs, rinsed, trimmed, and thinly sliced
1 (8-ounce) can sliced bamboo shoots, drained and rinsed
6 scallions, white parts and 4 inches of green tops, rinsed, trimmed, and cut into 1-inch lengths
6 ounces fresh spinach, rinsed and stemmed
2–3 cups cooked rice, hot

1. Rinse beef and pat dry with paper towels. Cut beef into $\frac{1}{2}$-inch slices against the grain. Combine stock, soy sauce, mirin or sherry, and sugar in a small bowl, and stir well to dissolve sugar.
2. Heat oil in a wok or large skillet over medium-high heat, swirling to coat the pan. Add beef, and brown well. Remove beef from the pan with a slotted spoon, and keep warm.
3. Add onions, mushrooms, celery, bamboo shoots, and scallions to the pan, and cook, stirring frequently, for 3 minutes, or until onions are translucent. Add sauce mixture, and bring to a boil. Cover the pan, and cook for 2 minutes.
4. Add spinach to the pan, stirring until it wilts. Return beef to the pan, and cook 1 minute. Serve immediately.

*Available in the Asian aisle of most supermarkets and in specialty markets.

Note: The dish can be prepared for cooking up to 6 hours in advance, and refrigerated, tightly covered. Also, it can be cooked in an electric skillet at the table. Preheat the skillet to 375°F.

Variation:
- Substitute 1 (14–16-ounce) package tofu for the beef; drain and cut it into ¾-inch cubes. The tofu needs no pre-cooking. Also substitute Vegetable Stock (recipe on page 57) for Beef Stock.

> To serve this dish authentically, place a portion of rice into a small bowl, and then ladle the beef mixture on top. It's also polite to hold the bowl close to your mouth, which makes using chopsticks easier.

Chapter 10:
(Almost) Guilt-Free $1 Goodies

Desserts should be part of kids' meals, but they are problematic, according to members of my Parents Panel. They all admitted to certain guilt about serving their family desserts of empty calories, but also used the promise of a sweet treat as a ploy to get kids to try new foods. They were all also acutely aware of all the chemicals and preservatives in commercial baked goods, and while those from special bakeries were made with wholesome, natural ingredients, it was at a high cost.

That's where the recipes in this chapter come into play. Almost all of them will alleviate guilt, as well as alleviate the strain on the budget. Most are made with fruit, and some include vegetables, too. While there is white flour in many cake recipes, there are also ones made with cornmeal and whole wheat flour. While you can't freeze a cake once it's been frosted, all of the basic cake recipes are freezable, too.

None of these recipes cost more than $1 per serving; most of them are more in the 50 cent range. And—like all recipes in the $3 Meals series—there are no convenience foods laden with chemicals. So there are many ways in which these goodies should be considered almost guilt-free!

SIZING UP THE SITUATION

It's always best to use the pan specified in a recipe. However, if that is not possible, the way to gauge which pan to substitute is to know the capacity of pans. It really makes no difference if the pan is round or rectangular, as long as the correct amount of batter is added.

Use a liquid rather than a dry measuring cup and water to measure the volume of pans. Use this method as well for novelty pans such as hearts and Christmas trees. Baking times and temperatures can change, however, with the dimensions of the pan. The best way to make adjustments is to look for a similar recipe specifying the size pan you are using.

Round Cake Pans	Volume
8 x 1½ inches	4 cups
9 x 1½ inches	6 cups

Angular Cake Pans	Volume
8 x 8 x 2 inches	6 cups
9 x 9 x 1½ inches	8 cups
9 x 9 x 2 inches	10 cups
9 x 13 x 2 inches	14 cups

THE CUPCAKE CONNECTION

Adults in swanky neighborhoods in Manhattan are learning what kids have known for generations—cupcakes are cool. These mini-cakes are all the rage at chic bakeries, and are even sold from street carts.

Cupcakes are generally baked at 350°F for 20–24 minutes, and the muffin cups have to be either greased (flouring is not necessary) or lined with paper liners. I'm in favor of the liners; they make the cupcakes less messy to eat, and they also keep them fresher. They're not very expensive, and kids like them, too.

While you'll find many cupcake recipes in this chapter, you may also have favorite cake recipes that you want to bake in this form. The only cake recipes that I don't think take well to cupcake form are dense cakes loaded with fruits. They tend to dry out because the baking time is too long. Here's a list of cake recipes and the number of cupcakes they make:

- Batter for 2 (8-inch) round layers makes about 18 cupcakes.

- Batter for 2 (9-inch) round layers makes about 24 cupcakes.

- Batter for an 8-inch square cake makes about 12 cupcakes.

- Batter for a 9 x 13-inch cake makes about 24 cupcakes.

Cinnamon Apple Fondue

Fondue makes a good dessert because it's all about the activity of dipping; in fact, it's so popular with my sister's grandchildren that they have a chocolate fountain. Think of a warm apple pie, fragrant with cinnamon. That's what this fondue is like, plus it's creamy too.

Yield: 4–6 servings | **Active time:** 5 minutes | **Start to finish:** 10 minutes

> 4 tablespoons (½ stick) unsalted butter
> ¼ cup all-purpose flour
> ½ cup heavy cream
> 1½ cups unsweetened applesauce
> ⅓ cup firmly packed light brown sugar
> ¾ teaspoon ground cinnamon

1. Melt butter in a 1-quart saucepan over medium heat. Reduce the heat to low, add flour, and cook for 2 minutes, stirring constantly.
2. Raise the heat to medium and whisk in cream, applesauce, sugar, and cinnamon. Bring to a boil, whisking until smooth. Reduce the heat to low, and simmer 1 minute.
3. To serve, transfer the fondue to a fondue pot or other pot with a heat source. Serve with hulled strawberries (halved if large), apple slices, donut holes, squares of waffle, cubes of angel food cake, cubes of pound cake, cubes of brownie, or sugar cookies.

Note: The fondue can be prepared up to 4 hours in advance and kept at room temperature. Reheat it over very low heat, stirring frequently, or in a microwave oven.

Variation:
- Substitute ground ginger for the cinnamon.

While there isn't really a Pillsbury Dough Boy or an Aunt Jemima, you can tell your kids that Johnny Appleseed was a real person. Named John Chapman, he was born in Massachusetts in 1774. Unlike the artistic depictions of propagating apples by tossing seeds onto the ground, in reality he started nurseries for apple tree seedlings in the Allegheny Valley in 1800. He had pushed as far west as Indiana and Illinois to establish groves of apple trees by the time he died in 1845.

Baked Stuffed Apples

A stuffing made with cookie crumbs, nuts, and raisins elevates this homey dessert to a new level of elegance. The Parents Panel told me that baked apples are always a hit, and they can be put into the oven as you sit down to dinner.

Yield: 4–6 servings | **Active time:** 15 minutes | **Start to finish:** 40 minutes

- 4–6 large baking apples, such as Jonathan, Northern Spy, or York Imperial
- 2 tablespoons lemon juice
- $\frac{1}{2}$ cup chopped walnuts, toasted for 5 minutes in a 350°F oven
- $\frac{1}{4}$ cup raisins
- $\frac{1}{4}$ cup pure maple syrup
- 4 tablespoons unsalted butter, melted, divided
- $\frac{1}{2}$ cup butter cookie crumbs
- $\frac{1}{2}$–1 cup unsweetened apple juice

1. Preheat the oven to 375°F. Core apples, cutting a cavity about 1 inch wide but not cutting through to the bottom. Peel skin around stem end to expose $2\frac{1}{2}$ inches of apple flesh. Rub cut surfaces with lemon juice to prevent discoloration, and prick skin with the tip of a paring knife to prevent apples from bursting.
2. Combine nuts, raisins, maple syrup, 3 tablespoons butter, and cookie crumbs in a small bowl. Stir to blend. Gently pack stuffing into cavities of apples. Brush exposed flesh of the apples with the remaining melted butter. Arrange apples in a shallow baking dish.
3. Pour $\frac{1}{4}$ inch of apple juice into the bottom of the baking dish. Bake apples, basting them once or twice with juices in the dish for the first 10 minutes. Continue to bake until apples are just tender when pierced with a metal skewer, about 25–30 minutes total time. Do not overbake; the centers of the apples should offer some resistance. Serve warm or cold.

Note: The apples can be baked up to 2 days in advance and refrigerated, tightly covered.

Variation:
- Substitute honey for the maple syrup, and substitute chopped dried apricots for the raisins.

Banana Cream Pie

Ripe bananas have a delicate flavor that is enhanced by the vanilla custard in which they're nestled in this easy-to-make pie.

Yield: 6–8 servings | **Active time:** 15 minutes | **Start to finish:** 9¼ hours, including 8 hours for chilling

> 1 (9-inch) Basic Crumb Crust (recipe on page 246) or purchased graham cracker crust
> ½ cup granulated sugar
> ⅓ cup cornstarch
> ¼ teaspoon salt
> 2 cups whole milk
> 1 cup heavy cream
> 3 large egg yolks
> 1½ teaspoons pure vanilla extract
> 2 tablespoons (¼ stick) unsalted butter, cut into bits
> 5 ripe bananas (about 1½ pounds total), peeled, and cut crosswise into ¼-inch-thick slices

1. Preheat the oven to 350°F. Bake crust for 12–15 minutes, or until golden. Remove crust from the oven, and cool completely.
2. While crust bakes, prepare filling. Whisk sugar, cornstarch, and salt in a medium saucepan to blend. Gradually whisk in milk and cream, then egg yolks and vanilla.
3. Whisk over medium-high heat until custard comes to a boil and thickens. Remove the pan from the heat, and whisk in butter. Scrape custard into a mixing bowl to cool for 1 hour.
4. Spread 1 cup custard over bottom of prepared crust. Top with ½ of sliced bananas, then 1 cup custard, covering bananas completely. Repeat layering with remaining bananas and remaining custard. Chill pie for a minimum of 8 hours, or until filling is set and crust softens slightly.

Note: The pie can be made up to 2 days in advance and refrigerated.

Variation:
• Substitute 1 quart sliced strawberries for the bananas.

Even bright green bananas will ripen within 3 days if placed in a paper bag with a few apples. Apples give off a gas that speeds the ripening process.

Peanut Butter Mousse Pie

Here's a dessert that kids as well as adults adore, and it's great in all seasons. The rich ganache and creamy peanut butter mousse are like a Reese's peanut butter cup on your plate.

Yield: 8–10 servings | **Active time:** 20 minutes | **Start to finish:** 4 hours, including 3 hours for chilling

> 1 (9-inch) Basic Crumb Crust (recipe on page 246) or purchased graham cracker crust
> 1 cup creamy peanut butter
> ³/₄ cup granulated sugar
> 1 (8-ounce) package cream cheese, softened
> 1 teaspoon pure vanilla extract
> 1³/₄ cups heavy cream, divided
> 8 ounces bittersweet chocolate

1. Preheat the oven to 350°F. Bake crust for 12–15 minutes, or until golden. Remove crust from the oven, and cool completely.
2. Combine peanut butter and sugar in a mixing bowl and beat with an electric mixer on medium speed until light and fluffy. Add cream cheese and vanilla, and beat well. In another mixing bowl, whip ³/₄ cup cream until medium-soft peaks form, and fold cream into peanut butter mixture until thoroughly combined. Refrigerate 30 minutes, or until slightly firm.
3. While mousse chills, chop chocolate into small pieces and place it in a mixing bowl. Bring remaining 1 cup cream to a boil over low heat in a small saucepan, and pour hot cream over chocolate. Stir until melted and thoroughly combined. Pour chocolate into pie shell, reserving about ¹/₃ cup at room temperature. Chill until firmly set.
4. Remove mousse from the refrigerator, and beat with an electric mixer on low speed for at least 5 minutes, preferably longer, until mousse is light and fluffy. Cover chocolate layer with peanut butter mousse, and distribute it evenly with a spatula. Place remaining chocolate in a pastry bag fitted with a small tip or in a plastic bag with small hole at one corner. Drizzle it decoratively over the mousse. Chill until ready to serve.

Note: The pie can be prepared up to 24 hours in advance and refrigerated, loosely covered with plastic wrap.

While we think of peanut butter as a timeless pantry staple, it's only about a century old. It was introduced at the St. Louis World's Fair in 1904 as a health food.

Carrot Cake

While making sweet foods with carrots dates back to the Medieval era, and is also part of Indian cuisine, the homey carrot cake with its traditional cream cheese frosting didn't become popular until after World War II. It's a fast cake to make, and it has universal appeal.

Yield: 10–12 servings | **Active time:** 20 minutes | **Start to finish:** 4 hours, including 2 hours for chilling

> 2 cups all-purpose flour
> 1 tablespoon ground cinnamon
> 2 teaspoons baking soda
> ½ teaspoon salt
> 1½ cups vegetable oil
> 1½ cups granulated sugar
> 4 large eggs, at room temperature
> 1½ teaspoons pure vanilla extract
> 1 pound carrots, peeled and shredded
> ½ cup sweetened coconut
> ½ cup finely chopped pineapple
> ½ cup chopped walnuts, toasted in a 350°F oven for 5 minutes
> 3 cups Cream Cheese Frosting (recipe on page 241)

1. Preheat the oven to 350°F; grease and flour 3 (9-inch) round cake pans with 1½-inch sides.
2. Sift flour with the cinnamon, baking soda, and salt, and set aside. Place vegetable oil, sugar, eggs, and vanilla in a mixing bowl and beat at medium speed with an electric mixer until well blended. Add flour mixture, and beat at low speed until just blended in. Stir in carrots, coconut, pineapple, and walnuts.
3. Divide batter among the prepared pans and bake for 35–40 minutes, or until cake begins to shrink away from the sides of the pan and a cake tester inserted in the center of each layer comes out clean. Cool cake layers on a rack for 15 minutes, then invert layers onto racks and allow them to cool completely. While cake cools, prepare frosting.

4. To assemble, place 2 overlapping sheets of waxed paper on a platter. Place 1 cake layer, flat side down, on the paper and spread with ³/₄ cup frosting. Repeat with second layer. Top with third layer and spread remaining frosting on the top and sides. Remove sheets of waxed paper. Refrigerate the cake for at least 2 hours before serving.

Note: The layers can be prepared 3 days in advance and refrigerated, tightly covered. The cake can be assembled 1 day in advance and refrigerated.

Here are some tips to make your cakes look prettier. Start with frosting that is partially chilled so it has some body to it, and ice the layers to ½ inch from the edge; this prevents too much dripping.

Zucchini Cupcakes

This is one of those sneaky desserts; it tastes sweet but it actually contains a serving of vegetables!

Yield: 12 cupcakes | **Active time:** 15 minutes | **Start to finish:** 45 minutes

2–3 medium zucchini
2 large eggs, at room temperature
³/₄ cup vegetable oil
²/₃ cup honey
1 teaspoon pure vanilla extract
1 teaspoon ground cinnamon
1 teaspoon baking powder
¹/₂ teaspoon baking soda
¹/₂ teaspoon salt
2 cups all-purpose flour
1 cup Cream Cheese Frosting (recipe on page 241)

1. Preheat the oven to 350°F, and line 12 muffin cups with paper liners. Grate zucchini through the shredding disk of a food processor, or grate it by hand through the large holes of a box grater. Measure out 2 firmly packed cups; use any additional for another purpose.
2. Combine eggs, oil, honey, and vanilla in a mixing bowl, and whisk well. Add zucchini, cinnamon, baking powder, baking soda, and salt, and whisk well again. Add flour, and stir until just combined.
3. Divide batter into the prepared cups, smoothing tops of cupcakes with a rubber spatula. Bake in the center of the oven for 20–24 minutes, or until a toothpick inserted in the center comes out clean.
4. Cool cupcakes in the pan on a rack for 10 minutes. Remove cupcakes from the pan, and cool completely before frosting.

Note: The cupcakes can be baked up to 2 days in advance and kept at room temperature in an airtight container. Once frosted, they should be refrigerated, loosely covered.

Variation:

- Substitute yellow squash for the zucchini, and ground ginger for the cinnamon.

Measure the oil in your measuring cup before measuring the honey; the honey will slide right out. If you're doing a recipe that doesn't call for oil, spray the inside of your measuring cup or measuring spoon with vegetable oil spray to achieve the same effect.

Chocolate Pumpkin Cupcakes

These really taste like chocolate cupcakes, but the pumpkin adds moisture as well as a delicately sweet flavor.

Yield: 12 cupcakes | **Active time:** 20 minutes | **Start to finish:** 45 minutes

> 6 tablespoons (3/4 stick) unsalted butter, softened
> 1/2 cup firmly packed dark brown sugar
> 1/2 cup granulated sugar
> 2 large eggs, at room temperature
> 1/2 cup canned solid-pack pumpkin
> 1/4 cup buttermilk
> 1/2 teaspoon pure vanilla extract
> 1/2 cup unsweetened cocoa powder
> 1 teaspoon baking powder
> 1/2 teaspoon baking soda
> 1/2 teaspoon salt
> 1/2 teaspoon ground cinnamon
> 1 cup all-purpose flour
> 1 cup Cream Cheese Frosting (recipe on page 241)

1. Preheat the oven to 350°F, and line 12 muffin cups with paper liners.
2. Combine butter, brown sugar, and granulated sugar in a mixing bowl, and beat at medium speed with an electric mixer to mix well. Increase the speed to medium-high, and beat until light and fluffy. Add eggs, 1 at a time, beating well between each addition and scraping the sides of the bowl as necessary. Beat in pumpkin, buttermilk, vanilla, cocoa powder, baking powder, baking soda, salt, and cinnamon. Reduce the speed to low, and beat in flour until just combined; do not over-mix.
3. Divide batter into the prepared cups, smoothing tops of cupcakes with a rubber spatula. Bake in the center of the oven for 20–24 minutes, or until a toothpick inserted in the center comes out clean.
4. Cool cupcakes in the pan on a rack for 10 minutes. Remove cupcakes from the pan, and cool completely before frosting.

Note: The cupcakes can be baked up to 2 days in advance and kept at room temperature in an airtight container.

Make sure you buy *solid-pack* pumpkin, which is a very thick puree of the vegetable, and not pumpkin pie filling; they're frequently shelved together in the baking aisle. The filling is looser and already spiced, and it will not work in this recipe.

Fox's Chocolate Beet Cake

My dear friend, Fox Wetle, is a master baker when she's not at her real job as a medical school dean. I ate this decadent cake a few times at her home and couldn't believe that it actually contained so many beets! Here's a truly guilt-free goodie.

Yield: 8–10 servings | **Active time:** 20 minutes | **Start to finish:** 2½ hours, including 2 hours for cake layers to cool

CAKE

1 cup vegetable oil, divided
2 ounces (2 squares) unsweetened baker's chocolate, chopped
2 (15-ounce) cans sliced beets, drained, or 1½ cups pureed cooked beets
3 large eggs
1½ cups granulated sugar
½ teaspoon pure vanilla extract
1½ teaspoons baking soda
1 teaspoon salt
1¾ cups all-purpose flour

ASSEMBLY

2 cups heavy cream
½ cup confectioners' sugar
1½ cups sliced strawberries

1. Preheat the oven to 350°F. Using the bottom of a 9-inch cake pan, cut out 2 circles of waxed paper or parchment paper. Grease 2 (9-inch) round cake pans, fit the bottoms with the waxed paper circles, and then grease the waxed paper.
2. Combine ½ cup oil and chocolate in a small microwave-safe bowl. Microwave on medium (50 percent power) for 1 minute. Stir, and repeat if necessary until chocolate melts. Puree beets in a food processor fitted with the steel blade or in a blender. Measure out 1½ cups puree, and use remainder for another purpose.
3. Combine eggs and sugar in a mixing bowl, and whisk until thick and lemon-colored. Add remaining oil, chocolate oil, vanilla, baking soda, and salt, and whisk well again. Add flour, and whisk until just

combined. Divide batter into the 2 prepared pans, smoothing the top with a rubber spatula.

4. Bake cake layers in the center of the oven for 20–25 minutes, or until a toothpick inserted in the center comes out clean. Cool layers in pans on a cooling rack for 10 minutes, then invert onto the cooling rack, and discard waxed paper. Cool cake completely.

5. Chill a mixing bowl and beaters well. Beat cream at medium speed with an electric mixer until soft peaks form. Add confectioners' sugar, and beat until stiff peaks form.

6. To assemble, place 2 overlapping sheets of waxed paper on a platter. Place 1 cake layer, flat side down, on the paper and spread with $1/4$ of whipped cream, and top with $3/4$ cup strawberry slices. Top with remaining layer, and spread whipped cream on the top and sides of cake. Arrange remaining $3/4$ cup strawberries on top. Remove sheets of waxed paper, and refrigerate cake until ready to serve.

Note: The cake can be made up to 1 day in advance and refrigerated, lightly covered with plastic wrap.

Variations:
- Substitute thinly sliced fresh peaches or bananas for the strawberries.
- Substitute My Favorite Chocolate Frosting (recipe on page 247) for the whipped cream and strawberries.

The best way to keep plastic wrap from sticking to a frosted cake is to create a "cage" around the cake with bamboo skewers. Insert skewers into the top and sides of the cake, and then loosely cover the plate with plastic wrap.

Classic Butter Pound Cake

I was horrified by both the cost and number of chemicals found in commercial pound cakes, so I devised this easy recipe. Serve it as the base for a sliced fruit dessert instead of making shortcakes. You can also toast the slices.

Yield: 8–10 servings | **Active time:** 15 minutes | **Start to finish:** 2 hours

> ¾ cup (1½ sticks) unsalted butter, softened
> ⅔ cup granulated sugar
> 3 large eggs, at room temperature
> 1 teaspoon pure vanilla extract
> ¾ teaspoon baking powder
> ½ teaspoon salt
> 1½ cups cake flour

1. Preheat the oven to 350°F. Grease and flour a 9 x 5-inch loaf pan.
2. Combine butter and sugar in a mixing bowl, and beat at medium speed with an electric mixer to mix well. Increase the speed to medium-high, and beat until light and fluffy. Add eggs, 1 at a time, beating well between each addition and scraping the sides of the bowl as necessary. Beat in vanilla, baking powder, and salt. Reduce the speed to low, and beat in flour until just combined; do not overmix. Scrape batter into the prepared pan, and smooth the top with a rubber spatula.
3. Bake cake in the center of the oven for 70–80 minutes, or until a toothpick inserted in the center comes out clean. Cool in the pan on a rack for 10 minutes, then invert onto the rack and cool completely.

Note: The cake can be made up to 2 days in advance and kept at room temperature, lightly covered with plastic wrap.

Variation:
- Substitute almond extract for the vanilla extract.

> The reason for bringing eggs to room temperature is so they blend easily with the butter and sugar. An easy way to do this is to place them in a mixing bowl and cover them with very hot tap water. Within 3 minutes the eggs will be at room temperature.

Cornmeal Pound Cake

I first encountered polenta cakes in Italy many years ago and liked the texture as well as the flavor that cornmeal added to the cake. The cornmeal also means that you're replacing some of the refined flour with a whole grain.

Yield: 4–6 servings | **Active time:** 20 minutes | **Start to finish:** 2 hours

- ³/₄ cup (1½ sticks) unsalted butter, softened
- 1 cup granulated sugar
- 3 large eggs, at room temperature
- 1 teaspoon pure vanilla extract
- ³/₄ teaspoon baking powder
- ½ teaspoon salt
- ²/₃ cup yellow cornmeal
- 1¼ cups cake flour

1. Preheat the oven to 350°F. Grease and flour a 9 x 5-inch loaf pan.
2. Combine butter and sugar in a mixing bowl, and beat at medium speed with an electric mixer to mix well. Increase the speed to medium-high, and beat until light and fluffy. Add eggs, 1 at a time, beating well between each addition and scraping the sides of the bowl as necessary. Beat in vanilla, baking powder, and salt. Reduce the speed to low, and beat in cornmeal and then flour until just combined; do not over-mix. Scrape batter into the prepared pan, and smooth the top with a rubber spatula.
3. Bake cake in the center of the oven for 75–85 minutes, or until a toothpick inserted in the center comes out clean. Cool in the pan on a rack for 10 minutes, then invert onto the rack and cool completely.

Note: The cake can be made up to 2 days in advance and kept at room temperature, lightly covered with plastic wrap.

Variation:
- Substitute almond extract for the vanilla extract.

> I don't believe in sifting dry ingredients; it's not necessary and it takes time and makes a mess. The flour is always added last so you can incorporate it into the batter gently to make the cake tender.

Maple Whole Wheat Bread Pudding

Adding whole grains to our diets is important, so I began devising a bread pudding recipe that would be delicious and also contain a serving of complex carbohydrates. Your kids will never know the difference.

Yield: 4–6 servings | **Active time:** 15 minutes | **Start to finish:** 1 hour

> $^1/_2$ pound whole wheat or whole grain bread
> 4 large eggs
> $^2/_3$ cup pure maple syrup
> $1^1/_2$ cups whole milk
> 1 teaspoon pure vanilla extract
> 1 teaspoon ground cinnamon
> $^3/_4$ cup raisins

1. Preheat the oven to 350°F, and grease a 9 x 13-inch baking pan. Cut bread into $^3/_4$-inch cubes.
2. Combine eggs, maple syrup, milk, vanilla, and cinnamon in a large mixing bowl, and whisk well. Add bread cubes and raisins, and push cubes down into custard mixture. Stir well, and allow mixture to sit for 10 minutes, stirring occasionally.
3. Scrape mixture into the prepared pan. Cover the baking pan with aluminum foil, and bake in the center of the oven for 30 minutes. Remove the foil, and bake for an additional 15–20 minutes, or until puffed and an instant-read thermometer inserted in the center registers 165°F.

Note: The bread pudding can be baked up to 2 days in advance; reheat it in a 325°F oven, covered, for 20–25 minutes, or until hot.

Variations:
- Substitute honey for the maple syrup, and increase the cinnamon to $1^1/_2$ teaspoons.
- Substitute fruit-only orange marmalade for the maple syrup, omit the cinnamon, and substitute dried cranberries for the raisins.

There are a lot of imposters out there in the whole grain market. Just as a product advertises "no trans fat" but then includes "partially hydrogenated" in the ingredient list, a product that's advertised as "100 percent wheat" may be far more all-purpose flour than whole wheat flour. To gain the health benefits of whole grains, the first ingredient on the list should be whole wheat or another whole grain, and the per-slice fiber content should be at least 3 grams.

Whole Wheat Date Nut Cookies

You'll enjoy these chewy cookies dotted with nuts and dates, and you'll enjoy knowing their nutritional content is high.

Yield: 3 dozen cookies | **Active time:** 15 minutes | **Start to finish:** 45 minutes

- 1 cup chopped walnuts
- 2 large eggs, at room temperature
- ²/₃ cup buttermilk
- ¼ pound (1 stick) unsalted butter, melted
- 1½ cups firmly packed light brown sugar
- 1 teaspoon pure vanilla extract
- ½ teaspoon baking soda
- ½ teaspoon salt
- 3 cups whole wheat flour
- 1 cup chopped dried dates

1. Preheat the oven to 350°F, and grease 2 cookie sheets. Bake nuts in a shallow pan for 5–7 minutes, or until toasted. Remove nuts from the oven, and set aside.
2. Combine eggs, buttermilk, butter, sugar, vanilla, baking soda, and salt in a mixing bowl, and whisk well. Add whole wheat flour, and stir until just blended. Fold in nuts and dates.
3. Drop dough by rounded tablespoonfuls onto the prepared cookie sheets, leaving 2 inches between cookies. Bake for 15 minutes for chewy cookies or 17 minutes for crispy cookies. Cool cookies on baking sheets for 10 minutes, then transfer to racks to cool completely.

Note: The cookies can be made up to 2 days in advance. Keep them at room temperature in an airtight container.

Variation:
- Substitute chocolate or butterscotch chips for the dates.

Don't want to buy a whole quart of buttermilk for one recipe? You can fake it. For each cup of whole milk, stir in 1 tablespoon lemon juice. Let it sit at room temperature for 10 minutes, and you'll have soured milk; it works the same way.

Cream Cheese Frosting

I put cream cheese frosting on just about everything; it's my favorite, and it's so easy to make.

Yield: 3 cups, enough for a 2-layer cake | **Active time:** 10 minutes | **Start to finish:** 10 minutes

4 cups (1 pound) confectioners' sugar
2 (8-ounce) packages cream cheese, softened
4 tablespoons ($\frac{1}{2}$ stick) unsalted butter, softened
$1\frac{1}{2}$ teaspoons pure vanilla extract

Combine confectioners' sugar, cream cheese, butter, and vanilla in a mixing bowl. Beat at low speed with an electric mixer until blended. Increase the speed to medium-high, and beat for 2 minutes, or until light and fluffy.

Variations:

- Decrease the amount of vanilla to $\frac{1}{2}$ teaspoon and add 1 teaspoon almond extract.
- Decrease the amount of vanilla to $\frac{1}{2}$ teaspoon, and add $\frac{3}{4}$ teaspoon ground cinnamon.
- Decrease the amount of vanilla to $\frac{1}{2}$ teaspoon and add 2 tablespoons frozen lemon juice or orange juice concentrate, and 2 teaspoons of grated lemon or orange zest.

Marshmallows

Some members of my Parents Panel thought making homemade marsh-mallows would be fun, while others instantly said it would be too much trouble. If you're in the thumbs-up group, you'll see how easy they are to make.

Yield: 20–40 marshmallows | **Active time:** 25 minutes | **Start to finish:** 12½ hours

3 (¼-ounce) envelopes unflavored gelatin
1 cup cold water, divided
1½ cups granulated sugar
1 cup light corn syrup
2 teaspoons pure vanilla extract
Pinch of salt
1 cup confectioners' sugar, plus extra for dusting

1. Sprinkle gelatin over ½ cup cold water in the bowl of an electric mixer fitted with the whisk attachment, and stir well. Allow gelatin to soften for 10 minutes.
2. Combine remaining water, sugar, corn syrup, vanilla, and salt in a small saucepan, and bring to a boil over medium-high heat, swirling the pan to dissolve sugar. Raise the heat to high, and cook syrup until it reaches 240°F on a candy thermometer.
3. Set the mixer on low speed, and slowly add sugar syrup to gelatin. Increase the speed to high, and beat for 12–15 minutes, or until mixture is very thick.
4. Sprinkle ½ cup confectioners' sugar on the bottom of a 9 x 13-inch baking pan. Pour in marshmallow mixture, smoothing the top with a wet rubber spatula. Sprinkle remaining ½ cup confectioners' sugar on top.
5. Allow mixture to sit for 12–15 hours, uncovered, or until it dries out. Invert pan onto a cutting board, and cut marshmallows into shapes. Dust shapes with additional confectioners' sugar.

Note: The marshmallows can be prepared up to 3 days in advance and kept at room temperature, loosely covered with plastic wrap.

Sugar syrup goes through various stages as it progresses from simple syrup to caramel, and 240°F is called the "soft ball" stage. The bubbles in the syrup are large and thick, and a bit dropped into ice water forms a ball that remains pliable when removed from the ice water.

Basic Piecrust

Another bakery item that costs very little to make at home is piecrust, and even if you never make a traditional pie, knowing how to make piecrust is important. It could lead to spicy empanadas or a savory quiche for lunch. Piecrust is essentially flour and fat, mixed with a little salt and water. The method remains constant; what changes is the proportion of ingredients.

Yield: Varies | **Active time:** 15 minutes | **Start to finish:** 15 minutes

PROPORTIONS FOR PIECRUST

Size	Flour	Salt	Butter	Ice Water
8–10-inch single	1⅓ cups	½ teaspoon	½ cup	3–4 tablespoons
8–9-inch double	2 cups	¾ teaspoon	¾ cup	5–6 tablespoons
10-inch double	2 ⅔ cups	1 teaspoon	1 cup	7–8 tablespoons

1. Combine flour and salt in a medium mixing bowl. Cut butter into cubes the size of lima beans, and cut into flour using a pastry blender, two knives, or your fingertips until mixture forms pea-size chunks. This can also be done in a food processor fitted with the steel blade using on-and-off pulsing.

2. Sprinkle mixture with water, 1 tablespoon at a time. Toss lightly with fork until dough will form a ball. If using a food processor, process until mixture holds together when pressed between two fingers; if it is processed until it forms a ball, too much water has been added.

3. Depending on if it is to be a 1- or 2-crust pie, form dough into 1 or 2 (5–6-inch) "pancakes." Flour "pancake" lightly on both sides, and, if time permits, refrigerate dough before rolling it to allow more even distribution of the moisture.

4. Dough can be rolled either between 2 sheets of waxed paper or inside a lightly floured plastic bag. Use the former method for piecrust dough that will be used for formed pastries such as empanadas, and the latter to make circles suitable for lining or topping a pie pan. For a round circle, make sure dough starts out in the center of the bag, and then keep turning it in ¼ turns until the circle is 1 inch larger in diameter than the inverted pie plate. Either remove the top sheet of wax paper or cut the bag open on the sides. You can either begin to

cut out shapes or invert the dough into a pie plate, pressing it into the bottom and up the sides, and extending the dough 1 inch beyond the edge of the pie plate.

5. If you want to partially or totally bake the pie shell before filling, prick bottom and sides with a fork, press in a sheet of wax paper, and fill the pie plate with dried beans, rice, or the metal pie stones sold in cookware stores. Place in a 375°F oven for 10–15 minutes. The shell will be partially baked. To complete baking, remove the weights and wax paper, and bake an additional 15–20 minutes, or until golden brown. Otherwise, fill pie shell. If you want a double crust pie, roll out the second half of the dough the same way you did the first half, and invert it over the top, crimping the edges and cutting in some steam vents with the tip of a sharp knife.

Note: The crust can be prepared up to 3 days in advance and refrigerated, tightly covered. Also, both dough "pancakes" and rolled-out sheets can be frozen for up to 3 months.

Variations:

- To create a fluted edge: Trim the pastry 1/2 inch beyond the edge of the plate, and fold under to make a plump pastry edge. Place your index finger on the inside of the pastry edge, right thumb and index finger on the outside. Pinch the pastry into V shapes, and repeat the pinching to sharpen the design.
- For an easy lattice crust: Cut 1/2–3/4-inch-wide strips of piecrust, using a pastry wheel or knife. Lay the strips across the pie in one direction, then in the other. Do not weave; however, fold edge of the bottom crust over the pastry strips and flute.
- For a shiny crust: Blend 1 egg yolk with 1 tablespoon milk or water. Brush over the top of the pie before baking.

Basic Crumb Crust

Crumb crusts are easy to make, and much less expensive than purchasing them ready-made in the supermarket. While graham cracker is traditional for sweetened cheese pies, key lime pies, and fruit pies, you can also use chocolate, vanilla, or any plain unfilled cookie to make a crust.

Yield: 1 (9-inch pie) | **Active time:** 10 minutes | **Start to finish:** 10 minutes

> 30 graham crackers or 2 cups graham cracker crumbs
> 6 tablespoons (¾ stick) unsalted butter, melted
> 2 tablespoons granulated sugar
> ½ teaspoon ground cinnamon (optional)

1. If using graham crackers, crush them into crumbs by breaking them into small pieces and chopping them in a food processor fitted with the steel blade using on-and-off pulsing, or place the pieces in a heavy resealable plastic bag and crush to crumbs with the bottom of a small skillet.
2. Combine crumbs, butter, sugar, and cinnamon, if using, in a mixing bowl, and mix well.
3. Spread mixture into bottom and up sides of the pie plate, pushing it firmly into place. Follow recipe directions for when to bake crust.

Note: The crust can be prepared for baking up to 2 days in advance and refrigerated, tightly covered.

The proportions of this recipe create a solid crust, but it's open to endless variation. Use ginger snaps, chocolate wafers, or any plain cookie. Use ginger, Chinese five-spice powder, or pumpkin pie spice as a flavoring.

My Favorite Chocolate Frosting

This easy frosting really delivers a powerful chocolate hit, and the sour cream balances its sweetness.

Yield: 2½ cups | **Active time:** 15 minutes | **Start to finish:** 45 minutes

6 tablespoons (¾ stick) unsalted butter
¼ cup whole milk
½ teaspoon pure vanilla extract
Pinch of salt
10 ounces bittersweet chocolate, chopped
¾ cup sour cream
1 cup confectioners' sugar

1. Combine butter, milk, vanilla, and salt in a medium saucepan, and place over medium heat, stirring frequently, until mixture comes to a simmer. Add chocolate, and whisk constantly over low heat until chocolate melts. Remove the pan from the stove, and allow it to cool until lukewarm, about 15 minutes.

2. Whisk in sour cream until smooth, then whisk in confectioners' sugar. Let stand for 10–15 minutes, or until thick enough to spread. If frosting thickens too much, reheat in a microwave oven on medium (50 percent) power for 30-second intervals until proper spreading consistency is reached.

Note: The frosting can be made up to 2 days in advance and refrigerated, tightly covered. Bring it to room temperature to reach the desired spreading consistency.

Variations:

- Add 1 tablespoon instant coffee granules to the butter and milk for mocha frosting.
- Substitute pure almond extract for the vanilla, and add ½ teaspoon ground cinnamon to the butter and milk for a Mexican chocolate frosting.

Appendix A:
Metric Conversion Tables

The scientifically precise calculations needed for baking are not necessary when cooking conventionally. The tables in this appendix are designed for general cooking. If making conversions for baking, grab your calculator and compute the exact figure.

CONVERTING OUNCES TO GRAMS

The numbers in the following table are approximate. To reach the exact quantity of grams, multiply the number of ounces by 28.35.

Ounces	Grams
1 ounce	30 grams
2 ounces	60 grams
3 ounces	85 grams
4 ounces	115 grams
5 ounces	140 grams
6 ounces	180 grams
7 ounces	200 grams
8 ounces	225 grams
9 ounces	250 grams
10 ounces	285 grams
11 ounces	300 grams
12 ounces	340 grams
13 ounces	370 grams
14 ounces	400 grams
15 ounces	425 grams
16 ounces	450 grams

CONVERTING QUARTS TO LITERS

The numbers in the following table are approximate. To reach the exact amount of liters, multiply the number of quarts by 0.95.

Quarts	Liter
1 cup ($1/4$ quart)	$1/4$ liter
1 pint ($1/2$ quart)	$1/2$ liter
1 quart	1 liter
2 quarts	2 liters
$2 1/2$ quarts	$2 1/2$ liters
3 quarts	$2 3/4$ liters
4 quarts	$3 3/4$ liters
5 quarts	$4 3/4$ liters
6 quarts	$5 1/2$ liters
7 quarts	$6 1/2$ liters
8 quarts	$7 1/2$ liters

CONVERTING POUNDS TO GRAMS AND KILOGRAMS

The numbers in the following table are approximate. To reach the exact quantity of grams, multiply the number of pounds by 453.6.

Pounds	Grams; Kilograms
1 pound	450 grams
$1 1/2$ pounds	675 grams
2 pounds	900 grams
$2 1/2$ pounds	1,125 grams; $1 1/4$ kilograms
3 pounds	1,350 grams
$3 1/2$ pounds	1,500 grams; $1 1/2$ kilograms
4 pounds	1,800 grams
$4 1/2$ pounds	2 kilograms
5 pounds	$2 1/4$ kilograms
$5 1/2$ pounds	$2 1/2$ kilograms
6 pounds	$2 3/4$ kilograms
$6 1/2$ pounds	3 kilograms
7 pounds	$3 1/4$ kilograms
$7 1/2$ pounds	$3 1/2$ kilograms
8 pounds	$3 3/4$ kilograms

CONVERTING FAHRENHEIT TO CELSIUS

The numbers in the following table are approximate. To reach the exact temperature, subtract 32 from the Fahrenheit reading, multiply the number by 5, and then divide by 9.

Degrees Fahrenheit	Degrees Celsius
170°F	77°C
180°F	82°C
190°F	88°C
200°F	95°C
225°F	110°C
250°F	120°C
300°F	150°C
325°F	165°C
350°F	180°C
375°F	190°C
400°F	205°C
425°F	220°C
450°F	230°C
475°F	245°C
500°F	260°C

CONVERTING INCHES TO CENTIMETERS

The numbers in the following table are approximate. To reach the exact number of centimeters, multiply the number of inches by 2.54.

Inches	Centimeters
½ inch	1.5 centimeters
1 inch	2.5 centimeters
2 inches	5 centimeters
3 inches	8 centimeters
4 inches	10 centimeters
5 inches	13 centimeters
6 inches	15 centimeters
7 inches	18 centimeters
8 inches	20 centimeters
9 inches	23 centimeters
10 inches	25 centimeters
11 inches	28 centimeters
12 inches	30 centimeters

Table of Weights and Measures of Common Ingredients

Food	Quantity	Yield
Apples	1 pound	2$\frac{1}{2}$–3 cups sliced
Avocado	1 pound	1 cup mashed
Bananas	1 medium	1 cup sliced
Bell peppers	1 pound	3–4 cups sliced
Blueberries	1 pound	3$\frac{1}{3}$ cups
Butter	$\frac{1}{4}$ pound (1 stick)	8 tablespoons
Cabbage	1 pound	4 cups packed shredded
Carrots	1 pound	3 cups diced or sliced
Chocolate, morsels	12 ounces	2 cups
Chocolate, bulk	1 ounce	3 tablespoons grated
Cocoa powder	1 ounce	$\frac{1}{4}$ cup
Coconut, flaked	7 ounces	2$\frac{1}{2}$ cups
Cream	$\frac{1}{2}$ pint (1 cup)	2 cups whipped
Cream cheese	8 ounces	1 cup
Flour	1 pound	4 cups
Lemons	1 medium	3 tablespoons juice
Lemons	1 medium	2 teaspoons zest
Milk	1 quart	4 cups
Molasses	12 ounces	1$\frac{1}{2}$ cups
Mushrooms	1 pound	5 cups sliced
Onions	1 medium	$\frac{1}{2}$ cup chopped
Peaches	1 pound	2 cups sliced
Peanuts	5 ounces	1 cup
Pecans	6 ounces	1$\frac{1}{2}$ cups
Pineapple	1 medium	3 cups diced
Potatoes	1 pound	3 cups sliced
Raisins	1 pound	3 cups
Rice	1 pound	2 to 2$\frac{1}{2}$ cups raw
Spinach	1 pound	$\frac{3}{4}$ cup cooked
Squash, summer	1 pound	3$\frac{1}{2}$ cups sliced
Strawberries	1 pint	1$\frac{1}{2}$ cups sliced

Food	Quantity	Yield
Sugar, brown	1 pound	2$\frac{1}{4}$ cups, packed
Sugar, confectioners'	1 pound	4 cups
Sugar, granulated	1 pound	2$\frac{1}{4}$ cups
Tomatoes	1 pound	1$\frac{1}{2}$ cups pulp
Walnuts	4 ounces	1 cup

TABLE OF LIQUID MEASUREMENTS

Dash	=	less than $\frac{1}{8}$ teaspoon
3 teaspoons	=	1 tablespoon
2 tablespoons	=	1 ounce
8 tablespoons	=	$\frac{1}{2}$ cup
2 cups	=	1 pint
1 quart	=	2 pints
1 gallon	=	4 quarts

Index

S

salad, Summer Taco Salad, 132–33
salad bar, shopping from, 14
sauces, dips, and glazes
   about: chili dips, 129; chili sauce, 91; cornstarch in, 209; freezing pizza sauce, 180; hoisin sauce, 203
   Asian Carrot Dip, 78
   Basic Pizza Sauce, 180
   Basic White Sauce, 33
   Glaze (for baked ham), 30–31
   Herbed Tomato Sauce, 32
   Hot Tex-Mex Sweet Potato Dip, 76–77
   Mexican Kidney Bean Dip, 75
saving money, 1–17
   comparing prices, 11
   cost per unit and, 11
   discount and bargain tips, 7–9. See also coupons
   following tips in book, 1–2
   ingredient compromises, x–xi
   in-store shopping strategies, 9–14
   mental preparation for, 16–17
   minimizing waste, 12–14
   other tips/habits for, 16–17
   planning before shopping, 2–3
   processed foods and, ix–x
   shopping list and, 3, 9–10
   supermarket alternatives, 14–16
   watching scanned prices, 12
seasoning tips, 81, 109, 125, 153
shopping tips. See coupons; saving money
Sloppy Joes, 100–101
smoothies
   about, 60–61; blender basics, 62; ingredients, 61; measuring ice cream and frozen yogurt, 63; modifying recipes, 61
   Banana and Peanut Butter Smoothie, 67
   Banana Colada Smoothie, 65
   Chocolate Banana Smoothie, 63
   Cinnamon Banana Smoothie, 64
   Creamy Strawberry Smoothie, 69
   PB&J Smoothie, 70
   Spiced Apple Smoothie, 68
   Tropical Pineapple Banana Smoothie, 66
snacks, 60–78
   about, 60; cutting granola bars, 73
   Asian Carrot Dip, 78
   Cranberry Granola Bars, 72–73
   Hot Tex-Mex Sweet Potato Dip, 76–77
   Mexican Kidney Bean Dip, 75
   No-Bake Peanutty Granola Bars, 71
   Super-Crunchy Raisin Granola Bars, 74
   See also smoothies
soups and stews
   about, 34–35; stocks, 34–35, 137
   Beef Stock, 56
   Beefy Vegetable Soup, 52–53
   Boston Baked Bean Soup, 40–41
   Cheddar Potato Chowder, 36–37
   Chicken Stock, 55
   Chili Soup with Beans, 50–51
   Indian Red Lentil Soup (Mulligatawny), 48–49
   Low-Country Fish Soup, 42–43
   New England Clam Chowder, 44–45
   New Mexican Pork and Hominy Stew (Pozole), 136–37
   Old-Fashioned Chicken Noodle Soup, 46–47
   Pork Stew with Mole Sauce, 134–35
   Potato Soup with Ham and Vegetables, 54
   Seafood Stock, 58–59
   Southwestern Bean, Squash, and Corn Soup, 38–39
   Turkey Chili, 128–29
   Vegetable Stock, 57
Southwestern foods. See Hispanic and Southwestern foods
spinach
   "Green Eggs and Ham" Pizza, 193
   Italian Sausage with Garbanzo Beans and Spinach, 170–71
   Pasta Shells Stuffed with Spinach and Ricotta, 142–43